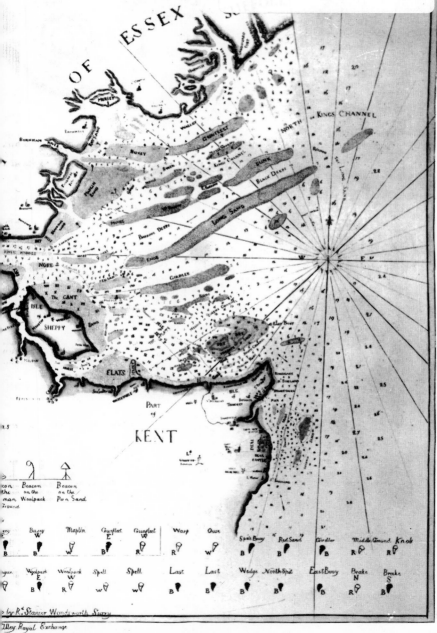

ROGUES' RIVER
Crime on the River Thames in the Eighteenth Century

Frank Martin

Ian Henry Publications
1983

ISBN 0 86025 874 2

Printed and bound at The Camelot Press Ltd, Southampton
for Ian Henry Publications, Ltd.,
38 Parkstone Avenue, Hornchurch, Essex RM11 3LW

CONTENTS

ILLUSTRATIONS

Bowles' print of the Thames above London Bridge c. 1760

Introduction

London was one of the mercantile capitals of the world in the 18th century. The Thames was like a giant funnel where hundreds of trade routes joined for the last 40 miles. It was also a lucrative hunting ground for thieves and a booming market for smugglers.

The Thames has passed its zenith as a vital trade route to and from London. Above Tilbury most of the up-river wharves are deserted and rotting; property developers are picking over the cavernous 19th century warehouses. The river is of more value to London as a water supply than a water way. The only river business that has flourished in recent years has been the tourist trade. Londoners, who either do not realise or would rather not be reminded that they drink its water, look upon the Thames merely as a creator of traffic jams or a flood danger. Yet in the 17th and 18th centuries it was sometimes impossible to see across the river at certain places because there were so many ships anchored or manoeuvering on the yellow-grey water. Daniel Defoe in 1724 counted 2,000 vessels in the Pool of London. The Thames was the only satisfactory way in which goods in large quantities could be transported to the warehouses of the City of London to satisfy the multiplying demands of England's flourishing 18th century trade. The river was twenty times cheaper than hauling cargo over the rough roads and tracks in carts.

Like the poor of the countryside who managed to live off the land, many of London's 18th century population could live off the river. Apart from seamen, there were lightermen, watermen, coopers, revenue officers, lodging house keepers, whores, bumboat operators selling goods to ships, lumpers unloading, inn keepers (who often acted as labour agents), crimps recruiting seamen, and many smugglers and thieves.

Patrick Colquhoun, an 18th century magistrate, estimated that a quarter of the City's population depended on the river in some way for their living: 10,800 of them dishonestly. It is the activities of those 10,800 that will most concern us. The underworld of the river, whether they were thieving, smuggling, or swindling, were taking far more from the revenue and the merchants along 40 miles of river than all the pirates on the high seas.

By the end of the 17th century England was one of the world's greatest trading nations. Her merchant adventurers had learned to overcome or take advantage of the succession of wars and treaties with the French, the Dutch and the Spanish. By the middle of the next century Pitt, when he was allowed by a far-from-enthusiastic George II, used England's naval and military power to defeat trading rivals. He saw French world trade as a threat to England and manoeuvered his forces abroad and his friends in Parliament to attack French trading interests wherever he could. Wolfe was encouraged to take great risks to drive the French out of Canada. The bulk of the sugar trade came with the capture of the sugar islands in the West Indies. Clive and Eyre Coote were allowed a free hand while they were successful in India. All this

2

pleased the City merchants who were enjoying the benefits of growing business opportunities and the interest on frequent government loans.

The fact that England was at war with someone did not seem to matter much where 18th century business was concerned, trade still went on in some way. During the Royal Navy mutiny at the Nore in 1797, the mutineers blockaded the Thames and were incensed to find that, while they were expected to endure the most appalling conditions on board His Majesty's ships for months or even years at a time, there was a regular traffic of merchant ships to and from our enemies. At that time the English navy was blockading Brest and the Texel off the Dutch coast where the French and Dutch fleets were preparing invasion forces; Admiral Jarvis and his Commodore, Horatio Nelson, were off Cadiz where they were about to defeat the Spanish fleet at the battle of Cape St.Vincent. We appeared to have few friends across the Channel, yet we managed to trade with Holland in the same year to the value of £2,211,362.0s.10d, buying corn, wine, gin, brandy, flax and dye stuffs; selling in return sugar, rum, tobacco, and rice. Similar business was done with France and Flanders: £1,015,017.19s, and Spain:- £947,759.17s.8d.

The 18th century saw the establishment of England's merchants as men of power and substance. From being intrepid adventurers of previous centuries they were becoming entrepreneurs who, while still not accepted in the salons of the true aristocracy, were managing to buy their way into the upper classes, and into positions where they could influence government. The Government, because of the need to finance an almost continuous succession of wars with one or more of its neighbours, was finding that it needed to call on credit from the trading companies. In return it granted and helped to protect near monopolies to trade in certain areas of the world, areas which were so rich in cheap labour, crops and other raw materials that it was akin to today's cliche of a licence to print money.

These companies so established themselves that they became like a branch of Government. The East India Company, while trading in India, was granted a Charter to maintain a standing army of over 20,000 men, presumably financed from profits. The West India Company was importing about 85,000 tons of sugar and $1\frac{3}{4}$ million gallons of rum per year from the Caribbean, while the Africa Company shipped 25,000 slaves across the Atlantic in 1700.

The fortunes of the London merchants and ship-owners were considerably improved by the Navigation Acts, the first of which was introduced by Oliver Cromwell in 1651, largely to combat the voracious Dutch, whose near invincible navy at that time was helping them to grab trade and colonies. Although England found it necessary to go to war with the Dutch three times in the next 22 years, the Navigation Acts proved to be a more long-lasting weapon in winning trade. They decreed that only British ships could trade with her colonies and certain specified goods, such as tobacco and sugar, must be shipped via London, no matter where they were eventually bound. This made England's colonies across the Atlantic virtually part of Britain, as far as trade was concerned.

In the early 18th century London was already accounting for 70% of English foreign trade, so the Thames had become one of the

4

busiest mercantile highways of the world. From the Nore to the Pool of London was like a 40 mile-long conduit where all the trading routes from India, China, the Americas and Europe finally came together to make their way to London. However, as a ship rounded the North Foreland and started to beat her way up the estuary she faced a number of obstacles, not least of which were the shifting sand and mud banks through which there was no dredged channel and few reliable charts. Large vessels would have to wait for high tides and favourable winds; they could take days to get up to Gravesend, where a customs officer came on board for the remainder of the journey to London. From Gravesend to the Pool of London the river twisted and turned between mud flats; the navigable channel offered a depth of less than twelve feet at low tide. Where the river swept round its steep bends it lost a third of its width and the windmills of the Isle of Dogs looked out on scores of small ships high and dry on the mud banks waiting for the tide to float them off. The big East Indiamen could only get up as far as Deptford where they discharged into barges and hoys. Smaller vessels would often have to anchor where they could upstream to await a berth. There was little regulation of anchorages, masters could drop anchor where they chose, blocking channels or risking going aground. Sometimes they waited for weeks to get to the quay side, for there were no docks, just various wharves north and south of the river.

In these conditions there were so many opportunities for every kind of wrongdoing involving the spiriting away of cargo, smuggling, and even piracy, that the merchants and the government found that the River Thames was rather like a sticky funnel through which their goods had to pass. Each contact the ship had with the shore or with the thousands of shore-based boats operating on the river meant that part of its cargo would, as it were, adhere to the sides of the funnel and be lost in some untraceable clandestine way.

How much illegitimate cargo was landed by the ingenious smuggling tricks described later, it is impossible to judge, but it represented a fortune and a flourishing business for the enterprising men of Kent and Essex. For instance, in the mid-1700s tea was available in London tea shops for about 5 shillings a pound, but the government-imposed duty on imported tea was sometimes as much a four and ninepence per pound according to which war they were trying to finance at the time. There could have been few tea merchants willing to survive solely on the return of three pence per pound, yet ninety out of a hundred families of the period were regularly drinking tea. The greater part of the tea consumed near the coast and the riverside had been landed in handy 40 pound 'dollops' which could be transported easily on pack horses or the backs of men to buyers who asked no questions.

While tea could be purchased in Europe for two shillings per pound and sold in England for at least five shillings, the temptation to bypass the customs dues was very strong indeed. A Parliamentary Committee enquiring into revenue frauds in 1784 listed East India Company figures which state that in the decade between 1772 and 1782 Europe imported thirteen million pounds of tea, but only consumed five and a half million pounds. The other seven and a half million pounds were smuggled illegally into Britain: this meant that half of Britain's entire tea consumption was smuggled.

The 18th century was the peak of lawlessness on the Thames. The lonely marshes and inlets of the Kent and Essex shores were not ideal landing places, but because of this they were sparsely populated and locals who knew the tides and mud banks could move about the twisting channels in their shallow-draught wherries landing contraband from smuggling cutters anchored out in the deeper water. Because of the flat terrain, especially in Essex, the chances of a Revenue Riding Officer being able to approach close enough to surprise them were remote.

Thieves and river pirates could take their pickings from hundreds of craft lying at anchor waiting for the tide. Wreckers could set up false lights to lead coasters on to the mud banks. Up river, among the tightly packed anchorages and the large shifting population of London, there were frequent opportunities to loot cargoes, steal from the wharves or from seamen who came ashore. Higher up the scale, there were frauds by merchants against the government, the Board of Customs – and each other.

On shore there was a ready market for anything plundered from ships. Whereas today things 'fall off the back of lorries', the 19th century aphorism would be 'dropped off a ship on the Thames'. There was an eager network of receivers, ranging from junk dealers who would buy ships' tackle to merchants who could handle large quantities of corn, sugar, coffee and spirits.

There appeared to be a dual standard of morality when it came to handling dishonestly acquired goods. Someone who would never contemplate robbery on shore would have no

7

scruples about taking part in the stealing of goods from ships. This was a condition brought about by years of smuggling.

Successive governments had tried to raise money by increasing revenue on imported goods to sometimes as much as a hundred per cent and more. This made smuggling very profitable and cheating the government out of revenue did not bother the conscience of too many people, a situation not unknown today. But the dividing line between goods which were smuggled and those which were stolen often became blurred. Lumpers and watermen who helped to land contraband could often be persuaded to assist in landing the odd hundredweight of sugar or coffee or help themselves to coal from one of the hundreds of unguarded lighters at anchor. A cooper could easily be found who would bore a hole in a cask so that a bladder of spirit could be drawn off and the cask re-sealed.

The river was a vast, floating warehouse containing everything that Londoners needed: food, clothes, hides, liquor, tobacco. There were also the luxury items like silk, china and spices that could find a market among the newly-rich aristocracy living in the smart west London villages of Mayfair, Westminster and Chelsea.

Until goods were unloaded and measured, there was no really accurate computation of quantities. Captains were supposed to go to the Customs House by Billingsgate to declare their cargo and swear various oaths that their ships complied with the Navigation Acts and what each cask and bale contained. As this was almost impossible to do accurately – and equally impossible to check – it coined the term 'custom house oath' for any oath or promise of doubtful sincerity.

8

There was no police force on the Thames until the West India Company formed their own Marine Police Force in 1797 in order to prevent huge losses of sugar and rum from their ships in the Caribbean trade. Before this security was in the hands of watchmen who were often old and in poor health. They were installed on board a ship or lighter and expected to watch over it, and sometimes several others, day and night. They slept when they could and rarely had any relief, therefore they were easily corruptible and intimidated by river gangs and dishonest seamen.

The only official security on an organised basis was supplied by the Board of Customs whose officers also found it prudent, or profitable, not to see too much thieving. Even conscientious Revenue Officers could only prevent a small part of the smuggling that occurred.

Those who did not look the other way were often subjected to violence and abuse, like Customs Officer Thomas Rowles who was stationed on board the *Lively Betsy*, while she was anchored off Hale Stairs in 1775. The ship had a cargo of sugar and was waiting for a berth. Her Master, Bennett Grey, ordered up a cask of sugar and had it broken open and about three quarters of a hundredweight transferred to another box for transhipment on shore.

This activity appeared to be going on before the eyes of Customs Officer Rowles who had been put on board the *Lively Betsy* to prevent such a happening as this. Officer Rowles, to use the words of his affidavit:

"...could not suffer this to be done, as it would be an injury to the Crown and to the Merchants whose property the said sugar was..."

However, the Customs Officer was in a dilemma which he and most of his colleagues often found themselves; he was facing a tough captain who had sailed his ship and cargo from the West Indies and was used to being the law on board his own vessel. So Officer Rowles report of the incident ends:

"... while endeavouring to prevent Captain Grey from proceeding I was seized by the collar and shaken very much and then had sugar flung in my face and was threatened with being flung overboard, by which means I was obstructed and hindered by the said Bennett Grey in the commission of my office on the said ship..."

There is also an agonising memo from Messrs. William Clark and John Brooks to their Lords of the Treasury. Mr Clark and Mr Brooks were sugar merchants in London and their report estimated that sugar to the value of £70,000 per year was being pilfered from their ships waiting to be unloaded on the Thames. Apparently the lumpers would go ashore for their meals with every available pocket and pouch full of sugar. Lightermen would contrive to miss the tide, so that they could anchor in mid-stream and off-load sugar to their friends who came in small boats in the night.

This was the Thames scene in the 18th century. The river was an integral part of of the trading prosperity of the nation, which would soon be prospering even more as the Industrial Revolution approached. Yet England was still in many ways operating with 15th and 16th century law enforcement. A man and a horse were expected to watch several miles of shore. Poorly manned Revenue cutters were being outsailed by well-equipped smugglers and near anarchy ruled on the tideway which had no adequate police force. As the second and third decades of the

10

19th century came, so police and the Coast
Guard were formed and the thieves began to find
life more difficult, but until then the underworld
river of the 18th century offered rich pickings.

London watchman and his lanthorn

Smuggling

By the 18th century smuggling had become a way of life for many Thameside communities. Beginning with the illegal exportation of wool, it developed into profitable import smuggling as successive governments imposed more customs tariffs.

Smuggling is the mythology of crime; writers have created a folklore around smugglers and their activities that has given the smuggler a paradoxical aura of honorable dishonesty. Readers seeking vicarious pleasure in the adventure involved in outwitting the law without actually violating some else's property have fed upon the myths of lovable rogues in striped jerseys and stocking caps hiding casks in caves.

This impression that smugglers are not quite as bad as other criminals is not entirely the fault of south coast publicity officers and novelists. The smugglers liked to call themselves 'free traders' and, although many of them were just opportunist criminals, there were others who genuinely saw themselves as traders persecuted by the Government. Smuggling would not have prospered in the 17th and 18th centuries if successive administrations had not imposed revenues which were often unfair, inordinately high, or impossible to administer.

It is difficult to determine when Thameside smuggling began. If we could trace the first regulation imposing a ban or a levy on the landing or export of something, it is likely that the first smuggler began work within hours of the issue of that regulation. The Saxon kings levied 'according to their needs', which was nothing more than a form of royal extortion. In the 10th century Ethelred, who was desperately trying to keep the Danes at bay by paying them ransoms, began charging a halfpenny on every boat that landed at Billingsgate. There were no doubt some who made surreptitious landings to avoid the $\frac{1}{2}$d levy.

It is hardly likely that these illegal landings were instrumental in Ethelred's un-readiness to repel the Danes, but he was probably one of the first to realise that it was easier to impose a tax than collect it.

In spite of the need to control the landing places and quays, it was soon realised that the imposition of revenues was a very lucrative form of taxation. It did not need a country-wide infrastructure of tax collectors trying to assess and then track down payment, with all the hazards of storing and transporting coinage. It was easier to set up a customs control at the landing and embarkation ports and wait for the goods to pass through.

Edward III, who was so often in debt that he once had to pledge his crown to the Mayor and Commonalty of London, imposed export taxes on wool on the pretext of 'needs of great business'. He also bought 20,000 sacks of wool at his own price and sold them to merchants, charging them considerably more. His officers imposed levies at will, calling them 'loans to the King'. Later rulers simplified things for them-selves by developing the practice of 'customs farming'. A local burgess or court favourite would pay to the Crown an annual fee and. in return, be granted permission to impose and collect customs revenue. In this way the Crown just collected the fees and left the 'customer', as he was called, to collect from the shippers in the best way he could. This method was so open to mismanagement and abuse that it probably helped to establish smuggling, rather than control it.

In mediaeval times there was no organised customs service to provide officers and any preventive measures were left to a very scattered deployment of land-based militia. In 1295 Sir Richard de Tany was custodian of the coast from Harwich to Brightlingsea in Essex. He had at his command eight soldiers at Harwich, four at St Osyth, four at Clacton and Frinton, all supervised by one soldier on a horse. However, they did manage to make some arrests for smuggling. In 1297 Henry Ardern of Colchester was convicted of sending uncustomed wool to Flanders in his vessel the *Fynch*. He was committed to prison and later released on promising to pay a twenty pound fine in installments. These installments were probably financed by further unauthorised trips to Flanders for there was a flourishing demand for English wool across the Channel.

Early smugglers found it more profitable to take things out of the country rather than bring them in. Henry Parish was a fisherman from Barking Creek. In 1608 he was suspected of carrying more than just fish in his boat. He was making a large profit transporting people. He was associated with Henry Kiene who lived in a small lane off Tower Street in London. Kiene was known as a 'transporter of people'. For ten pounds he would hire Parish to take persecuted Catholics out of the country. Jesuit priests and young men on their way to Catholic seminaries at St Omer and Douai would make their way to lonely spots on the Essex marshes at Dagenham

14

or Tilbury and there Parish would pick them up on his way down-river and sail them to places across the Channel. Parish would then increase his income by loading up with bales of illegal Catholic literature or messengers who did not wish to advertise their arrival in England.

The principal factor in the establishment of smuggling as a way of life for thousands of the inhabitants of the south and east coasts was the severe regulation on the export of wool. Overcoming the restrictions became a vast conspiracy to smuggle wool out of the country involving farmers, labourers, fishermen and many of the landed gentry of Essex and Kent.

Sheep farming and the production of woollen garments was the most widespread and important industry of mediaeval England. Whole towns owed their livelihood to the wool industry. Many of the magnificent country towns and cathedral-like churches of East Anglia were built with money donated by prosperous wool merchants. But, although England produced the finest wool, it did not have the monopoly of cloth manufacture. The European cloth-making industry was centered on the valley of the Schelde in Flanders which had a reputation for producing the highest quality cloth. Unfortunately, the wool from European sheep was too coarse for the Flemish weavers, they needed the fine English fleece.

Kings and governments from the Middle Ages had been bullied and bribed by the powerful wool merchants and clothing makers of England to regulate the export of wool and even ban export completely. This was to maintain the price level and protect the English cloth making and spinning industry; it also ensured high profits for the merchants. However, these profits did not go to the wool growers, the sheep farmers. The merchants, because of their influence at Court and with governments, were able to buy cheaply and sell dear.

Staple ports were established from time to time through which all wool exports were supposed to pass, the most important of these being Calais when it was under English rule. No matter from where the wool was shipped and what was its eventual destination, it was supposed to pass through Calais, where it was weighed and priced by merchants who had a Charter from the Crown to deal in wool. In this way they were able to control the price and the supply of wool to their advantage.

The losers in this cosy cartel between the wool merchants, the clothiers and the government were the actual wool growers. Sheep farmers of Kent and Essex wanted to be able to sell their wool in a free market, but in order to do so they had to break the law and resort to smuggling.

It was not difficult for farmers to quietly shear their sheep, pack the fleece into bundles that could be slung either side of a horse and then lead the horses across country paths at night to where French or Dutch shallops would be waiting. There were also plenty of farm labourers willing to work for a few shillings a night driving a pack train down to Reculver, the Medway or between the creeks and mud flats of the Essex marshes.

The penalties for those who were caught were very severe, but the chances of discovery were not very high and local Justices were often sympathetic and sometimes directly involved with the smugglers and, although they could impose a death penalty, only a few ever suffered so severely. So, over the years between the 13th and 17th centuries, wool smuggling became a way of life for many Essex and Kent men; they acquired their own title, they were known as 'owlers'. They acquired skills in avoiding discovery and, where necessary, in fighting their way out of tough situations. They built up a closer affinity with the Flemish merchants who bought their wool and the French and Dutch boat owners than with authority in London.

In 1696 the government began to see that their policy of death penalties, transportation and other severe punishments was not effective, so slightly milder penalties were introduced together with an Act of Parliament designed to curb wool smuggling on the coast. Farmers living within ten miles of the coast were ordered to register their wool crop within three days of shearing and to store it in specified places. Everyone trading in wool within fifteen miles of the coast had to give sureties that they would not re-sell their wool to any other person in the fifteen mile zone. This was to overcome the organised marketing system that the owlers had built up by dealing direct with the Continent.

These regulations sounded good in Parliament, but they had one outstanding flaw; they could only be administered by a large number of Revenue Officers and the Government did not want to go to such an expense. King William III had barely subdued the Scots and the Irish and was at war with the French, who were supporting the exiled King James II. He needed money from the customs revenues, but was not willing to spend too much on its collection. By this time wool smuggling out of the country had rival profitable activities: the duties on tea, spirits, tobacco and many other items had opened up a

17

vast market for the import smuggler. Goods were being landed by many ingenious ways to avoid discovery by the inadequate Customs Service.

To use modern jargon, the Customs Service was supposed to be self-financing and this was often taken literally. In a later semi-official guide for Customs Officers, the old position of Searcher was described thus:

"... appointed for their assistance in the business of the customs without doors to see that no goods were imported or exported without the due payment of duty, and not being allowed any salary were to take the moiety of all forfeitures and seizures for their pains..."

So he was entitled to half of all he seized, which no doubt ensured he remained diligent, but how much could one man seize, bearing in mind that he may be on the deck of a smuggling cutter facing a crew of armed men? Hence, most prudent searchers only discovered caches of unguarded contraband or the odd half-anker of brandy being rowed ashore by an aged boatman.

The customs cruisers were also hampered by tight purses and by the systems of payment which were only adequate if the cruiser happened to catch a smuggler running a large cargo, for the master and crew of customs cruisers relied very much on the income from the sales of seized goods.

Until the 1790s most cruisers were contracted to the Board of Customs by private contractors who were paid by the weight of their vessel. One record quotes four shillings and sixpence per ton per month with a share of the seizures, or losses, with the Crown. There is also a record of the Board writing to the Collector of Colchester Customs setting out the terms for the use of a cruiser in 1783, in which they would pay the Master £50, the Mate £30, Mariners £15, and a boy £8 per annum. There would also be an allowance of nine pence per day and one shilling per month for each person for 'fire and candles'. They also sternly point out that the allowance for tallow should not exceed one pound per ton in two calendar months and that if the ship should happen to be destroyed by "fire, storm or any other unavoidable accident, or if she should be taken and destroyed by enemies or otherwise" half of the cost must be borne by the commander "allowing a reasonable deduction for fair wear and tear".

On another occasion the Colchester Collector was authorised to make a payment to two widows whose husbands had been killed while they were serving in the cruisers:

"... that the widow Schooling has no child living, but is left with child, and that the widow Butcher has one living and is big with another, you may pay the said widows the following sums being the usual allowance given on like occasions viz:

Widow School for herself	£7 .. 10	.. 0d
More on account of her being with child	£1 .. 10	.. 0d
Widow Butcher for herself	£7 .. 10	.. 0d
More for her child and for being with child	£3 .. 0	.. 0d"

This appeared to be the standard annual payments made to widows and orphans, there were also similar payments for injuries, like £10 per annum for the loss of an arm or a leg, or eighteen pence a day to an injured waterman "while his condition remained serious".

Although they were called cruisers the customs boats were often quite modest sloops or smacks; the largest on the Thames was the

19

Repulse of 210 tons based at Colchester, but most were 60 or 70 tons, good for the shallows and creeks, but not fast enough or strong enough to match the bigger smuggling cutters in open water. Towards the end of the century the smugglers were using well armed vessels of 200 or 300 tons. A Parliamentary report prepared in 1784 was very indignant at the audacity of the smugglers:

"...The most considerable of these vessels are able to make seven or eight voyages in a year; the largest of them can bring in one freight the enormous quantity of three thousand half ankers of spirits and ten or twelve tons of tea, besides several other articles to a con-siderable amount; the strength of some of them is such as to enable them to bid defiance to the Revenue cruisers, some of which have recently been insulted, fired upon and beat off, and others have either been seized and carried off or scuttled and sunk. In other instances the crews of the smuggling vessels have made prisoners of some of the officers of the Revenue, and have kept them aboard at the time of landing valuable cargoes. It is also a practice for the large armed vessels to take under their convoy the small defenceless craft which are employed in the same pernicious traffic."

The practice was for the larger smuggling vessel to be 'mother ship' to smaller ones, so that when they came near the coast, goods could be loaded into the smaller craft which could negotiate the quieter channels, slipping in with the tide. There were many people on the Kent and Essex shore who owned small sailing craft that could easily be converted to a form of ancient galley propelled by a large number of oarsmen. This meant that, if there was an alarm

20

or fear of discovery, they could all bend to and out-run any pursuers. It also meant that the profile of the vessel could be very low without a sail, so that they could creep in between the tufty marshes and reeds without the tell-tale sail showing above the top of the banks.

Stealth was the best method for running goods. If any discovery could be avoided while landing contraband, then the distribution of the goods was that much easier and safer. There were some favourite places for smugglers on both Essex and Kent shores of the estuary where a skilled boatman with a lifetime's knowledge could choose one of the meandering waterways that snaked through the marshes, and quietly guide his boat with sacking-covered oars to a landing spot. However, the right tides and the 'dark moons' sometimes did not coincide. This was when the tub line came into use. Half anker casks of brandy or other spirit would be strung together on a line and hung along the gunwale of the boat. Before reaching the low water line, the string of casks would be thrown overboard and weighted to sink to the bottom. A piece of fine line would be attached and to this line was fixed either a feather or a cork or, maybe, a bladder which would float to mark the spot for someone to return and retrieve the casks by dragging a grappling hook over the spot marked by the float. It is highly probable that many people ended up drinking a brandy and salt water mixture as a result of leaking casks spending too long on the bottom of the Thames, but a lot of the spirit was so raw and strong that the contamination probably did not notice. Some smugglers would always carry the casks strung together in a tub line, so that if a customs cutter approached, the casks could be rapidly thrown overboard in the

21

hope that they could be retrieved later.

Successful smugglers always tried to land their goods on dry land and get away without discovery. On the Kent side there were more navigable channels to landing places than on the Essex shore. After rounding the North Foreland. you could choose the exposed, but lonely, beaches under the cliffs near Reculver or beat up to Whitstable where there was more river traffic to hide among. Faversham offered a ready labour force to get the goods inland. Daniel Defoe in his *Tour through the Whole Island of Great Britain* refers to Faversham thus:

"... I know nothing else this town is remarkable for, except the most notorious smuggling trade, carried on partly by the assistance of the Dutch, in their oyster boats. and partly by other arts, in which they say, the people hereabouts are arrived to such a proficiency, that they are grown monstrous rich by that wicked trade; nay even the owling trade (so they call the clandestine exporting of wool) has seemed to be transposed from the Rumney Marsh to this coast. As to the landing of goods here from Holland and France, such as wine and brandy from the latter and pepper, tea, and coffee, callicoes, tobacco, and such goods, (the duties of which being very high in England, had first been drawn back by debentures) that black trade has not only been carried on here as I was informed, but on both sides the river. on the Essex as well as the Kentish shores..."

Reaching Faversham was sometimes hazardous, the revenue men based at Whitstable watched closely for any likely smuggler trying to slip into the river Swale, so some would try to hug close to Sheerness Cliffs and try to creep past Sheerness garrison into the Medway where they could soon be lost among the many inlets or into Long Reach past Queenborough and back to Faversham from the 'narrow end'. Another cosy landing place was Yantlet Creek, which divides All Hallowes from the Isle of Grain, or did before it was silted up. In the 18th century it was a good anchorage for vessels up to 80 tons and any customs men approaching over All Hallowes marshes could soon be spotted.

Today the area around All Hallows and the Isle of Grain is busy with holiday caravans, oil installations and a power station, but two centuries ago there were just scattered farms and small fishing communities. The slightly undulating terrain would hold pockets of mist in the early mornings of spring and autumn which would cling to the waterways. A Revenue man would need sound knowledge of the area and a fair amount of courage to ride the coastline without finding himself lost in the marshes or outnumbered by smugglers.

The Essex shore was more tricky because of the large expanse of the Maplin Sands. Those who knew the area could use the tide to slip into Havengore Channel on the flood and get into the Roach. where places like Paglesham, Great Stambridge, and Rochford were good smugglers' haunts. It is said that the tower of Rochford church was used as a store place for gin and brandy, and a cavity under the pulpit was known as 'the magazine'.

Another favourite landing place on the Essex shore was Leigh, which was on the decline as a port in the 18th century, but could still offer enough water for brigs and small trading schooners to anchor close in to the shore among the oyster dredgers. The watermen of Leigh made their living either as fishermen or smugglers, usually a little of each, although there was some smuggling going on that was very well organised. John Loten, Collector of Customs at Leigh in the 1780s, estimated in one of his reports to the Board of Customs that there were two vessels of between ten and thirty tons smuggling from Leigh. A local inn called the Peter Boat was burned down in the 19th century and it was found to have a secret room in the cellar connecting directly to the shore.

There are the usual stories of smuggling characters which have been passed on and, in the passing, have gained colour until they have been beyond recognition as the truth. There is one, William 'hard apple' Blyth of Paglesham in Essex, who has gained a reputation as a notorious smuggler. This reputation seems to stem from the memoirs of John Harriott, who lived in Great Stambridge near Rochford. Harriott tells a number of stories about Blyth: the most likely to be true is of the occasion when Harrriott was on the French coast returning from a trip to Europe. He was seeking transport home to Essex. Unlike today's frustrating tumble through air or ferry terminals, the 18th century traveller had to adopt more freelance travel arrangements. Harriott found an inn near Dunkirk frequented by English seamen. He entered, making sure that the customers saw him empty his pistols, they then accepted him as one of themselves, i.e. smugglers. They were from Kent, but they said that William Blyth from Paglesham would be arriving later. So Harriott spent the evening drinking toasts to the Revenue for, as Harriott pointed out to the Kent smugglers, without the revenue laws they would not be in business. When Blyth arrived they set sail for England and Harriott was eventually landed a mile and a half from his own door at Great Stambridge.

Harriott also tells of the time that Blyth was captured by a customs cutter and was in chains when they ran aground and he was asked to use his knowledge of the tides to re-float the cutter. There were also stories of Blyth killing a bull with his bare hands and eating glass and outwitting customs men by getting them drunk.

Whether these tales are even partly true is impossible to tell. However, there was a William Blyth who lived at Paglesham; when he died in 1830 aged seventy-four he was described in the Parish Register as 'former oyster merchant', which was the sort of profession that would almost certainly involve him in trips across the Channel. There is no record of Blyth ever being charged with any smuggling, in fact, he was a member of the Parish Council for a number of years and, for a time, was Parish Overseer. The rates book lists him as having a house and a shop in Paglesham. Another nice, but possibly apocryphal story, is that the scarcity of parish records is due to the fact that Blyth used the pages of the records to wrap butter in his shop. But the stories may be half true, for another notorious smuggler in the area who owned a profitable smuggling cutter was William Dowsett – and William Dowsett was Blyth's father-in-law. The probability is that Blyth, as an oyster merchant, was involved in smuggling, but he was also a respected member of the Parish Council. Either his exploits were not as colourful as Harriott would have us believe -- or they were the sort of activities which made someone a worthy citizen at that time.

Not all the smuggling was carried out by local boatmen. In October, 1772, Customs Officer Thomas Lee, together with two other customs

boatmen, boarded a Flemish brig called the
Antwerp Paquet from Middleburgh while she was
anchored off Leigh. She was not as foreign as
she sounded, for it was a common practice for
ships to be registered as Flemish or French or
Dutch in order to allay the suspicions of the
Revenue. Very often these ships had English
masters and English crews who claimed to be
French or Flemish. but could speak only English.
The *Antwerp Paquet*'s Master was John Hodgekins
and he objected most strongly when customs--man
Lee began to rummage the ship. His objections
were understandable for flasks of geneva and
stone bottles of other wine were found in the
sand ballast and in other boxes in the forecastle.
As was the practice at that time, the customs
officer marked all the goods with the broad
arrow to signify that they had been seized. He
began to take the seized liquor to the side where
he intended to load it on to his customs boat.
The Master of the *Antwerp Paquet* was so
enraged that he took up an axe and threatened
to cut the revenue boat loose and cast the
officer into the sea. When he saw that he was
not going to intimidate the customs men, he
began swinging his axe at the stone jars and
flasks in order to smash them. The whole party
could do nothing but watch the gin and wine
trickle across the deck and soak into the ballast.

Most of the run goods landed at Leigh
were quickly carried inland, where there appeared
to be a greater population of drifters than on
the Kent side. Gypsies and highwaymen mingled
with soldiers home from the wars who formed a
community of thieving squatters on places like
Daws Heath. a couple of miles inland from
Leigh. or on Tiptree Heath. which was said to be
a more or less permanent fair of smuggled or

stolen goods; the contraband was hidden in rough holes on Tiptree Heath. The holes were dug in the ground to form a small cave, which was then covered with timber and bracken; these holes then served as a store and a verminous home for the shifting population.

The other convenient landing place on the Essex side of the estuary was on the west side of Canvey island, where Hole Haven Creek cuts deep into Fobbing Marshes. The innkeepers of Fobbing and Corringham were always well supplied with tax-free liquor. When, today, all you can see on the horizon of this Essex shore are scores of fuel tanks and a lacework of refinery pipes, it is hard to imagine slow-moving carts with sack-muffled wheels and lines of ponies loaded with packs and casks on their way inland before the sun came up.

Today it is difficult for us to appreciate that the best means of fast travel over short distances on water in the 17th century was with the aid of manpower. A regulation was introduced in 1721 to try to prevent smugglers using boats that could carry a large number of oarsmen. It stipulated that no boat could operate with more than four oars. This did not appear to be too successful, because there is a later directive from the Commissioners of Customs to the out ports warning that boats were being built in London of gigantic length with only four rowlocks – but it was clear that twelve others could be easily fitted when needed.

An illustration of the effectiveness of multi-oared galleys occurred in 1752; the East Indiaman *Essex* arrived in the river at the end of a trip from China. The Gravesend customs cutter, under the command of Captain John Sturgeon, escorted the *Essex* to an anchorage in Long

Reach, just above the spot where the Dartford Tunnel now crosses the Thames. As soon as the East Indiaman dropped anchor Mr Sturgeon saw a large number of men begin unloading boxes and parcels into a long-boat; his estimate, possibly exaggerated, was that there were sixty men at work unshipping boxes.

Sturgeon lowered his boat and summoned up the assistance of two six-oared galleys from Grays and Greenhithe, but by this time the smugglers were under way and making for the northern bank of the river. The Revenue gave chase and were able to catch up with the smugglers, but they were beaten off vigorously:

"... we were repulsed by the sailors on board the said boat being so many and armed with long poles loaded with iron pikes, and with handspikes with which they dangerously wounded Norton Flower and another preferable waterman who were then in one of the six oared galleys..."

But the Revenue man continued to chase the smugglers who landed at Rainham Ferry. The pursuit then continued on land and the smugglers, or some of them, were eventually caught at Dagenham:

"... where we seized from about twenty of them severally parcels of china and India goods, but that the greatest part of the goods which were unshipped and put on board the long boat were carried away by the other sailors..."

So reads the affidavit sworn by Captain Sturgeon on 25 June, 1752. It appears from this that a large party of at least twenty men was able to row a long boat so fast as to outstrip the revenue's six-oared galleys to such a degree as to allow them time to land at Rainham, unship the goods and presumably escape on foot as far as Dagenham a few miles away.

There were also attempts to limit the ownership of vessels fast enough to outsail the customs cutters. One needed a licence to operate a fast sea-going cutter. Cutters in the 17th century were very much like sloops, fore and aft rigged, but with more sail area and less free-board, they sat lower in the water. But the essential point is the length and positioning of the bowsprit: a cutter had a movable bowsprit which could be run out to accomodate more sail. Sloops were supposed to have a fixed bowsprit, but many had cunning arrangements that enabled the crew to extend it to put on more sail when trying to escape the Revenue. This extra bowsprit was illegal and the owner risked losing his ship and incurring a fine if he was caught. But, of course, the idea was not to get caught, to have a boat fast enough to have just that few knots over the Revenue cutters which were often built to plod about in all weathers.

As the 18th century progressed, the old methods of farming out the customs collection had died out in favour of Collectors of Customs and Controllers of Customs appointed by the Board of Customs in London. But some of the old 'Customer' posts were still occupied by men in what amounted to sinecures. They continued to draw fees, but did nothing. It was still an age of patronage and a customs post was often given as a reward for services rendered to the Crown. Once the post had been conferred on someone he held on to it until death. There was an Inspector of Cloth Exported and Petty Custom Outward long after the cloth duties had been abolished and, from 1775 to 1784, the average income from this man's activities was £64 per annum. There was also a Surveyor of Subsidies and Petty

Customs, who continued to draw a salary of £1,800 per year long after his duties had ceased, he also had the services of a deputy clerk at £180 per year to help him do his non-existant job!

The new breed of professional officers did not always bear close examination; Commissioner Musgrave complained in 1782 that some officers of the out ports had been appointed:

"... from country foxhunters, bankrupt merchants, and officers of the army and navy without the least knowledge of the business of the Revenue and too late in life to acquire it, so that they are totally unfit to keep good order in the port or to be the representatives of the Board which they are required to be in many respects..."

The actual preventive officers, the men who had to be in the front line, sailing the estuary and river in all weathers and patrolling the shore night and day, were also a mixed bunch. Some were ex-sailors and soldiers, some were ex-smugglers, or even practising smugglers, for the methods of recruiting the so-called 'inferior officers' was sometimes haphazard. The job was a thankless one and could attract unsuitable characters who were either lazy or were bigger crooks than the people they were supposed to be apprehending. Although men were not supposed to be posted to areas where they once lived, they soon became known if they were stationed in a small area. It was a great temptation to share in the running of goods and then 'seizing' some and collecting a reward for the seizures. It was also easy for an officer to have run goods in his possession and forget to mark them with the broad arrow. If he was discovered with the goods he could claim that they were a

30

seizure and he was about to deposit them at the customs depot.

Many of the problems concerned with dishonesty of officers was due to the policy of not employing enough officers on a full-time capacity. The policy was to take on 'glutmen' or 'extra officers' on a casual basis when needed. They had little allegiance to the service and often saw to make some extra money by taking bribes or assisting in the running of goods.

Another troublesome aspect of the part-time officer system was the engagement by the Government of privateers in time of war. These privateers carried letters of marque making them temporary Royal Navy ships. They were usually small ships which the navy would employ on inshore duties or as tenders to the fleet, plying back and forth with messages and stores to and from the war ships engaged in blockading the French or Dutch ports. If the privateers wanted to take risks and engage the enemy they were free to do so and, of course, keep anything they captured. Many of them also found that, as privateers, they could claim certain privileges when it came to submitting themselves for customs examination. Certain privateer captains, some of whom were rather dubious mercenaries anyway, realised that they could engage in smuggling goods to and from Europe and make money safely by trading with the enemy rather than fighting him.

An added complication for the Board of Customs was that some of the privately owned customs cruisers which were hiring themselves to the Board could also take out letters of marque to allow them to act as privateers, so they were sailing for two masters – the Admiralty and the Board of Customs.

The Commissioners were not happy with this situation. They sent a directive to the out ports:

"... several commanders of privateers and tenders belonging to His Majesty's ships of war who have commissions from the Board, frequently go over to Holland and other foreign countries and in the course of their voyage either by meeting ships at sea or otherwise, take on board great quantities of goods as well customable as prohibited and run them on the coasts in the several ports and harbours of the Kingdom... and you are to inform the commander and every seaman of every such vessel that neither the commission from the Admiralty nor their being employed as tenders in the service of the Government, nor their having a deputation from this Board does exempt their being rummaged by the officers of His Majesty's Customs..."

However, it was difficult for the Board of Customs to refuse permission for the commanders of customs cutters to engage in privateering in time of war, but their unease is apparent in a letter to the Collector of Customs in Colchester dated November, 1780. They were giving permission for Daniel Harvey, captain of the cruiser *Repulse*, to take out letters of marque. They could hardly refuse, for England was at war with both France and Spain at the time, as well as being engaged with the newly-independent America; but they did point out:

"... we shall not consent to bear any part of the expense for any damages that may be sustained in engagements where no seizure shall be made for breach of revenue laws and you are to enjoin in the strictest manner not to quit his station under the pretence of looking for captures..."

32

Their unease is understandable for only three months earlier the *Repulse* had run aground on the coast near Calais by:

"... the wilful misconduct or negligence of the crew unconstrained by stress of weather or the superior force of the enemy, not only out of the limits of their duty but on a foreign coast..."

Obviously once a cutter left its home port it was difficult to keep tracks on where it was patrolling and the temptation was for the Master to make for an area which would show him the greatest profit, legitimate or otherwise.

One of the opportunist masters was George Box of the cutter *Kite*, formerly based at Dover. Mr Box took temporary leave from the Customs Service and hired his ship and crew to the Navy. This meant that he had to leave the Dover area and found himself acting as a fleet tender off the Nore on the north Kent coast, where, because it was virtually the next-door area to his of Dover he was no doubt well known. The Nore was patrolled by the customs service based at Rochester, who may have been a little jealous of the *Kite* operating in their patch.

The cutter *Success* was sent from Rochester to investigate Mr Box and his crew while they were anchored off Herne Bay. A boarding party, under Second Mate Thomas Gibbs, boarded the *Kite* and demanded the right to rummage for run goods. Box refused, saying he had a commission as a privateer, and no one should rummage his ship except by force. The customs men then noticed that:

"... all the hatches thereof were locked and barred and the same guarded by men and mariners thereof with firearms and cutlasses, and being inferior in numbers and force were obliged by such numbers and threats to desist from making such search..."

The customs men went back to their cutter, probably muttering threats that 'we'll be back', for on the next day they did come back, possibly with more men and better armed, for Second Mate Gibbs demanded access to the hold and:

"... that on refusal he would, at the hazard of his life, break open the hatches..."

But he did not have to use force, for the privateer opened his hatches and let the customs men rummage the ship for run goods. Not surprisingly, they found nothing. What happened between 20 and 21 March, 1779, remains un-recorded; there was probably a late night boat trip ashore to Faversham from the *Kite* - if so, why were the customs men not watching? Perhaps they were taking part.

The land-based Revenue officers were not so free to roam, if they were conscientious they had a diffult and, sometimes, dangerous job. The position of Riding Officer was described thus:

"... are appointed to reside at or near some particular places on the sea coasts, and have certain districts alloted to them, some part whereof they are to visit daily in order to discover any vessels hovering on the coast with design to land or take on any un-customed goods, which they must, by all possible means, en-deavour to prevent; and in the case of fraudulent landing or shipping of any goods to seize them with the vessels, boats, etc..."

For this task they were given a horse and a cutlass and the semblance of an ill-fitting uniform. The Riding Officer was probably a familiar and conspicuous figure in the locality. Even today the access places to the Kent and

34

Essex riverside are limited; there are vast expanses of reed-covered marsh into which a man can sink to the knee at each step. The bridle paths were confined to the more stable stretches a few feet above water level. In good weather a rider could be seen from afar. The only cover was the frequent marsh mist which aided the smuggler as well as the officer. As the smugglers preferred to work hardest during the dark winter months, the unfortunate Riding Officer frequently found himself plodding through deserted mud flats heavy with frost or riding before dawn into howling arctic wind scything in from the North Sea.

By the 17th century the descendants of the old owlers had centuries of smuggling expertise behind them. In mediaeval days they were content to sell their wool to French and Dutch middle men, but the modern 18th century owlers could see the advantage of selling their wool direct to the continent and then using the profits to buy tea, spirits, silks, and tobacco, which they then brought back to the thinly populated coasts of the Thames estuary. Farm horses were often working in the fields by day and were then quietly led off to the shore at night to wait for the shaded lantern signal from a shallow draught wherry as it was silently paddled ashore on the tide. The brandy or geneva was usually packed in handy four gallon half ankers strung together in pairs, so that they could be carried over the shoulders of a man or slung across the back of a horse. Tea was also packed in 'dollops' of about ten pounds which could be easily handled. The silk and Indian cotton was in bales sewn up in oil skin to protect them from damage by sea water.

It would be a brave Riding Officer who

would dare to challange a smuggling party as it was making its way from the shore in strength; but eventually the goods had to be dumped somewhere to wait carriage inland· this was when the customs officer was safer in discovering the contraband, but not always. Henry Baker, Riding Officer in the County of Kent, was on patrol on 2 June, 1783, when he found twenty-five half ankers of geneva and brandy hidden in a hedge on the road between Herne and Reculver: probably left by smugglers who had brought the casks inland from the coast the night before.

The procedure when an officer found run goods was to immediately put the goods under some form of guard, not an easy task for someone who could not rely on the honesty of the locals. Officer Baker went to a nearby farm to borrow a horse and cart and proceeded to load the twenty-five half ankers into the cart. As he was wearily driving his load back to his home, he was overtaken by William Inge and William Tappenden, both from the village of Dunkirk near Broughton. Inge and Tappenden were on horseback and had probably been summoned by the farmer from whom Officer Baker had borrowed the cart. They were very belligerent and, according to Baker·

"... threatened to knock my brains out..."

He was left on the roadside as the two smugglers drove off with the cart.

This episode was witnessed by Peter Hall, described as a yeoman, and William Adams and Simon Horn, described as labourers. They later signed affidavits describing the incident, but they did not come to the assistance of Officer Baker. The smugglers left behind three casks of geneva: could it be that they were for the three on-lookers? It is more than probable, because later that night the smugglers called at the house of Henry Baker and offered him two casks of brandy. This was an illustration of the strange blend of bribery and force often evident in the relationship between smugglers, the local residents, and the Revenue. In this case, Officer Baker did not take the bribe, otherwise he would not have reported the incident, but one wonders how many other bribery offers were accepted by officers. There are many affidavits by officers who have first been offered bribes, then on refusal the smugglers have resorted to violence.

There is also evidence that the smugglers could control the locals by intimidation, if bribery failed. In a letter to the Surveyor General of Riding Officers of Kent, another officer details his difficulty in getting evidence:

"... I have done all that is in my power to induce the person that informed me, but he is a farmer and lives at Reculver, and he says he is affraid ye gang will bourn down his house and barn if he should discover any of them, and so says everyone that I have interceded with on this afear, they all say that as there is no force in ye country, the smugglers will do as they pleas with them if they affrount them..."

There seems to have been scant respect shown towards Revenue Officers by the smugglers. An excise officer, Thomas Sears from Rochester, was on patrol with Riding Officer Kingsford Sharp:

"... in order to seek for and seize smuggled goods according the duty of the said office..."

when, about two o'clock in the morning, just as they were approaching Chatham Lines, where a company of dragoons was billetted, they saw two

37

men ahead of them, carrying what looked like half anker casks. As the men realised they were being followed, they threw down the casks and stood beside them. Officer Sears' deposition, in its 18th century equivalent of police jargon, goes on:

"... This deponent [Sears] said to his said companion [Kingsford Sharp] "hello here they are" and immediately the said Kingsford Sharp received a most violent blow from a very long bludgeon and with which Duncan Miller, late of the parish of Chatham in the County of Kent, struck him on the head, and at the same time Amos Hearnden, the other of the said two men said to this deponent [Sears] "Damn your eyes you shall have the same as the other" and immediately with a very long bludgeon he made at the deponent and aimed several blows at him and at the same time saying "Keep off Sears"..."

It is interesting that the smuggler knew the name of the officer in spite of it being two o'clock in the morning. The customs man in a local area must have been somewhat like a local policeman of today having his movements closely monitored by the criminal fraternity.

Sears warded off the blows from Hearnden with his sword, but at the same time he also had in his other hand a loaded pistol that he pointed at Hearnden threatening to fire if the smuggler "did not desist from obstructing him". Hearnden shouted back:

"... shoot and be damned, damn your eyes, if you do shoot hold your pistol straight or else you are a dead man..."

Meaning, presumably, that because the pistols of the day were only loaded with one shot it had to be an accurate shot or the

38

smuggler would then beat him to death with his stick before he could re-load. Officer Sears' deposition goes on:

"... I said 'I do not want to shoot you without cause but Mr Sharp (who was calling loudly for assistance) will be murdered unless I go to him, let me reason with you' and the said Amos Hearnden answered: 'If you attempt to go I will knock your brains out' or words to that effect which were repeated when this deponent again threatened to shoot him, but which however this deponent abstained from doing and retreated backward from the same Amos Hearnden until he came near the sentinel then on duty near that part of the lines who called out the sergeant and his guard from the guard-house and who upon learning that this deponent was an officer of the Excise interfered to the assistance of this deponent and took the said Amos Hearnden into custody..."

This was a stroke of good fortune for the belligerent Hearnden, for things began to get worse; Sears' deposition goes on:

"... and then this deponent looking about saw the said Duncan Miller [the other smuggler] leave the said Kingsford Sharp and run off with two of the said half ankers which this deponent immediately followed and as he came up struck him with his hanger [sword] on the head telling him he should not have them, but the said Duncan Miller saying that he would, immediately struck at this deponent with his stick which missed him. The said Duncan Miller then threw down the said two half ankers and then holding up his said stick put himself into a fighting posture saying 'Damn you, I'll serve you as I did the other' and this deponent [Sears] said: 'If you do not deliver up the goods I'll fire at you', but the said Duncan Miller continued aiming blow after blow at this deponent with the said bludgeon which he held in both hands and which being very long kept this deponent from reaching him with his said hanger..."

What the dragoons from the guardhouse were doing while all this was going on is not mentioned. They seem to have had little enthusiasm for getting involved for the sergeant of the guard had only called them out when he realised that a customs man was being attacked. The deposition concludes:

"... being afraid of being killed or at least maimed like the said Kingsford Sharp who was then totally disabled from helping this deponent owing to the very violent wounds and bruises which he had received from the said Duncan Miller, he, this deponent in defence of himself and of the said Kingsford Sharp and in order to complete the examination and the seizure of the said casks or half ankers did fire his said pistol at the said Duncan Miller, the ball from which passed through the said Duncan Miller and killed him..."

Although this is only one side of the story, it demonstrates that the smugglers were prepared to stand and fight for about eight gallons of spirit. Another incident at Whitstable is an illustration of the anarchy and brute force surrounding the smugglers' activities; in this case they were strong enough to match the law, such as it was. William Fosten, Master of the customs cutter based at Leigh in Essex, relates that he was anchored in Whitstable Bay on a June evening. At eight o'clock he saw a ship called the *Fox* sail into the bay with two smaller boats astern of her. As she anchored another small boat left the shore and was rowed alongside. Men began unloading tubs from the *Fox* into the small boats. This was in full daylight on a summer's evening.

As the small boats with their contraband were being rowed ashore, Mr Fosten with four of his own mariners went ashore and ran along the beach to where the smugglers were by now beginning to unload the boats. As the customs men approached the crew of the *Fox* leaped into one of their boats and tried to row back to their ship. Mr Fosten ran into the water and grabbed hold of the gunwale to try to prevent them rowing away, but his hand was forced off the side and the smugglers escaped back to the cutter leaving the other two boats with their contraband on the beach.

Fosten and his men mounted guard on the boats which, because of the ebb tide were now high and dry upon the shore. He sent two men back to the cutter for reinforcements and they returned with nine men, some muskets and cutlasses. The party then stood guard, waiting for the tide to re-float the loaded boats, so that they could be impounded and taken back to the cutter. However, the smugglers had some accomplices ashore, for at one o'clock in the morning:

"... a large party of men to the number of eight or more whom this deponent [Fosten] hath no doubt were smugglers and belonged to Whitstable aforsaid, armed with great clubs and cutlasses came up to us and on being asked what they wanted they replied: 'You buggers, we will soon tell you what we want', this deponent then discharged a pistol at them and attempted to discharge a second but it snapped and would not go off, and this deponent then ordered his men to fire which they did but some of their pistols also misfired and this

41

deponent having no weapon to defend himself with, one of the gang made at him but this deponent beat him off by throwing both his pistols at his head..."

This bears out the threat of the previous incident, with the pistols of the day you needed to be lucky first time, otherwise they were useless, except as missiles. Fosten was knocked down and his party overpowered. One of the smugglers came up to Fosten as he lay bleeding on the beach and stood over him with a drawn cutlass that he pushed against Fosten's chest, threatening to run him through. He was persuaded not to by another of the smugglers, who Fosten recognised as Stephen Hodges, Master of the *Ox*, another Whitstable ship.

The smugglers made off with the casks, leaving one boat and nine casks of spirits behind – could this have been another attempt at a bribe? The defeated customs men made their way back to their cutter with the small amount of seized goods and a fair amount of cuts and bruises. Mr Fosten's deposition ends with a sad resume of their losses and injuries:

"... having lost one musket, three pistols, and five cutlasses belonging to the cutter and two other pistols the property of the deponent. And this deponent further saith that in consequence of the wounds and bruises he received from the said smugglers he was under the care of Mr Warner of Gravesend, Surgeon, and Mr Geraud of Faversham, Surgeon, for some time and was incapable of doing his duty for one month..."

It is not possible to trace the outcome of these fights except for the word 'transportation' written in the margin of Mr Fosten's deposition, which is among the King's Bench Records at the

42

Public Records Office. So it appears that someone may have been eventually apprehended and
spent the next seven years in the colonies or,
more likely, on one of the prison hulks moored
in the Thames and Medway (see Chapter 6).

It appears that officers were more anxious
to seize goods than they were to arrest smugglers. This was an understandably safer course of
ac:ion, but it may also have been because the
officers were frequently dealing with people they
knew. The population of the Essex and Kent
riverside was not the suburban multitude it is
today, they were more stable village communities
of friends and relatives. An order from the
Board of Customs to the Collector at Colchester
in 1745 shows concern that not enough smugglers
were being arrested. Apparently the Lords of the
Admiralty had complained to the Duke of Newcastle, the Secretary of State, that they were
worried about smugglers carrying information to
the enemy – France was helping the Jacobites
prepare an invasion of Britain:

"... officers of the customs suffer
the smugglers to escape after they are taken.
The Commissioners direct you in the strongest
manner to excite all the officers of your port to
use their utmost endeavours when they make any
seizures to apprehend the smugglers which it is
always their duty to do, but more immediately
as the informations the smugglers carry to
France are very prejudicial to His Majesty's
Service..."

The risks involved in trying to arrest the
smugglers were often in vain for, due to the
closely knit communities, they frequently
received light sentences or were acquitted by the
magistrates and juries, who may well have been
good customers of the smugglers.

James Collier, who was Surveyor General of Riding Officers in Kent in the mid-1700s, complained to the Board of Customs in one of his reports that magistrates would not exercise their powers against persons 'lurking on the coast' and would not convict men found with tea in their houses and that, on one occasion, his officers caught men with run goods in their possession at Birchington, but local magistrates would not prosecute.

There seems to have been a reluctance to prosecute unless the smugglers were caught in the act of transporting the goods or if officers were hurt. Sometimes the brutality of the smugglers went too far and outraged public opinion so much that a real effort was made to hunt down the criminals, as at the fracas at Bostall Hill, near Whitstable, in 1780.

Officer Nicholson, Supervisor of Excise, assisted by eight dragoons, was involved in a battle with a large party of smugglers who completely overwhelmed Nicholson and the dragoons, killing two of the soldiers and wounding two others.

A smuggling cutter had been driven into Whitstable Bay by bad weather and had to unload its cargo. They were discovered by Nicholson, who seized three thousand gallons of geneva and had it loaded into carts to be transported to a customs depot at Maidstone. The party had just left Whitstable and was winding its way slowly up Bostall Hill with the dragoons escorting when they were attacked by about fifty men.

The attackers were determined to succeed and did not bother to argue, they opened fire with numerous pistols, killing two dragoons and wounding others. The *Kentish Gazette* of 23

February, 1780, said that the whole of the gin, except two tubs, was carried off on the back of the attackers, which was a convincing illustration of the numbers in the group. A good many shots must have been fired on this occasion, for shots passed through the hats and clothes and grazed the legs of other dragoons.

The smugglers then took the 3,000 gallons of gin back to the ship in Whitstable Bay, re-loaded it and she sailed off as the weather improved.

This sort of mob law was too much, even for those times, and a great fuss was made to find the culprits; a reward of £5 was offered for any information which led to capture. The result was an indication that not all smugglers were lovable rogues, for someone claimed the £5 by naming 17-years-old John Knight and six others. At the trial it was only the unfortunate Knight who was in the dock, the others were listed as 'at large'. It is possible that Knight, who was a simple youth, had been sacrificed by his compatriots in order to quieten down the hue and cry. He was found guilty and sentenced to be taken to the parish of the crime and publicly hanged. His body was then to hang in chains at the place of the ambush.

It appears that Knight did take part in the raid, for the indictment at his trial reads:

"... did make an assault on one John Aitken with a certain gun to the value of five shillings then and there charged with gunpowder and leaden bullet which the said gun, he, the said John Knight with both his hands then and there had and held to and against the said John Aitken then and there feloniously, wilfully and with malice aforethought did shoot off and discharge..."

The *Kentish Gazette* reported his execution on 13 March, 1780:

"... His behaviour at the place of execution was such as became his unhappy situation, and just before he was turned off begged of the spectators to take warning how they assist the smugglers... he was drawn in by persuasions of those who knew better and were more interested..."

John Knight was clearly involved in the ambush on Bostall Hill and it was possible that he fired one of the fatal shots as the indictment claims, but it was also probable that his friends were content to see him 'turned off' if it meant that they would not be hunted too rigorously.

Smuggling into the counties of Kent & Essex was clearly a profitable 18th century activity. So profitable for those who were well organised as to make it possible to employ what amounted to private armies of up to three hundred men as porters or 'batmen', as the guards were called.

There are many figures on the extent of smuggling, some are of doubtful reliability, especially those offered by pamphleteers trying to prove a point. But it is certain that the amount of tea and spirits being illegally imported during the 18th century was huge. The Commissioners of Revenue reported to the Treasury that for the year 1773 in the counties of Suffolk, Essex, Kent and Sussex they siezed 54,000 pounds of tea and 123,000 gallons of brandy, and they admit that this was only a small percentage of the total smuggled goods. The Commissioners also admitted to a Parliamentary Committee in 1784 that they were only equipped to detect frauds and small illicit landings from merchant ships and coasters. The

Committee also heard that the smugglers were so well organised that they had a system of riders collecting orders rather like the present day sales representatives. There was also a system of insurance for buyers who were afraid of losing their goods to the Revenue before they were delivered.

The usual price for smuggled goods by the time they reached London was about two-thirds of the goods imported legally. To those who lived near the shore or the ports of the estuary it was even cheaper. Parsons had casks left at the vicarage door, farmers who allowed their horses and carts to be used at night were rewarded with ten pound 'dollops' of tea left at the farm gate.

A good deal of the blame for the widespread smuggling must rest with the successive governments who were ready to impose customs levies whenever they needed extra money. Next to the land tax, the customs duties were the best form of government income. Whereas land tax fell only on those who owned land, a customs levy was spread more evenly. There was also the consideration that many of the landowners were not without influence in government and at the Royal Court. It was politically easier to add threepence a pound to tea than to go to the landowners.

The result of the governments' readiness to keep dabbling with the customs revenue often meant that some of the goods were attracting a 100% levy before they reached the consumer: this was especially so of tea. The East India Company and the Dutch East India Company were shipping large quantities of tea into Europe. It was still looked upon as more of a luxury than it is today, but the public's taste for it was growing

47

rapidly. This did not displease the East India Company, who enjoyed the preferential treatment of paying less than the duty charged to other importers.

The greater became the popularity of tea, the more the government was tempted to impose extra duties. Many of the duties were imposed for a specific debt, usually concerned with the almost continuous state of war which England found herself in during most of the 18th century. So a particular item of expense was financed by an impost of a penny or so on tea for a period of two or three years. This also served to re-assure the bankers who made the loan; they could see from where their interest and capital was coming back. But it also helped the smuggling trade to flourish. In 1784 shopkeepers had to pay four shillings and threepence for legally purchased bohea tea, yet it was on sale in many shops for only five shillings a pound. Brandy had a duty of nine shillings a gallon, but could readily be purchased on the coast for three shillings a gallon.

George Bishop, writing a pamphlet in 1782, claims that there were one thousand, six hundred and seven licenced public houses in the county of Kent and four thousand, eight hundred and twenty-one unlicenced ones:

"... where the poor labouring people assemble to drink without being seen by their masters or the parish officers..."

How Mr Bishop managed to count all those unlicenced houses he does not tell, but, even allowing for exaggeration, there was probably more smuggled liquor consumed than the legitimate variety. There is a story that, in Essex, gin was so plentiful that people cleaned their windows with it.

A more reliable source of figures is a

report from the Commissioners of Excise to the Treasury dated 1778, saying that smuggling had increased to such a degree that:

"... in some Collections the greatest part of the fair traders and dealers in tea and other excisable commodities imported have been obliged to discontinue their business and the consumption of the country to a greater or lesser degree has been supplied by the smuggler..."

They also point out that the gross product of the duties on tea from midsummer, 1773, to midsummer, 1775, was £1,118,820.3s.11½d, but in the subsequent two years, when tea drinking was increasing, the revenue was down to £934,396.12s.2½d. They also point out that, while tea could be purchased in Holland for thirteen pence per pound and sold in London for over four shillings, smuggling would continue. This is the nearest to criticism of the Government that they get, but the Parliamentary Committee that reported on smuggling in 1784 allows itself to be more direct:

"... The great and infallible remedy towards the prevention of frauds against the Revenue is undoubtedly to be fought only in the reduction of duties: it is natural that the increase in smuggling should bear a proportion to the temptation. The profits presented to adventurers by the high duties upon tea, foreign spirits and tobacco, certainly gave birth and give support to the expensive and piratical systems under which the smugglers have lately acted..."

An event which brought a large number of the 'piratical adventurers' out of their Thameside bolt-holes was the arrival in the Thames of an East Indiaman laden with tea, silks, china, and spices. These were the big ocean-going liners of the 18th century, although

49

they are quite small by today's standards. They had probably been on the seas for months and their cargoes represented the investment of a fortune by their owners, but how much extra cargo they carried on behalf of the officers and crew is impossible to determine. If the stories of how much smuggling was involved are only half true, it is difficult to understand how there was room for legitimate cargo.

The Parliamentary Report mentioned earlier contains a graphic account of the arrival of an East Indiaman:

"... It is well known that when ships are expected from the East Indies, smuggling vessels and boats of various sizes and descriptions and from every part of the coast cruise for them in the British Channel, and carry on a constant traffic with them, from the entrance to the Channel to their arrival in the Thames. As soon as the laden ships arrive at their moorings, the place near which they lie become the resort of smugglers, and resemble a public fair: and the river is crowded with boats watching hourly opportunities to convey goods out of every part of the ship..."

The Board of Customs was well aware of the temptations offered by a well-laden East Indiaman for the smuggling population and they did their best to prevent the situation described above.

Early in the century there was a system whereby up to eight tidesmen would be sent down from Gravesend to Deal to board the ship as she arrived in the Roads and stay on board until she reached her berth at Blackwall. In the 1750s this was discontinued because the tide-waiters, making their way to Deal, very often tarried too long at inns and did not arrive in too good a condition. There were cases of tide-

50

waiters being 'sorely incapacitated' from sea-sickness on the trip up the estuary. It was also rather a thankless job to go on board a ship as a snooper and have to spend a few days watching the crew and rummaging for contraband, while at the same time, being reliant on the ship for your food and sleeping accomodation. There are stern warnings from the Commissioners to the out-port officers pointing out that Masters of in-coming ships should provide accomodation for officers of the Revenue according to their station, and that failure to do so would result in a fine. No doubt those officers who were over-officious in their searches for run goods were subjected to an uncomfortable trip.

The practice of putting tidewaiters on board at Deal was eventually abandoned because it was of little practical use. It encouraged collusion between Revenue Officers and the crew, and did not result in many seizures. In its place a customs galley was deputed to sail in convoy with the East Indiaman, and customs sloops from the Medway hovered in Sea Reach and Lower Hope Reach until the ship dropped anchor at Gravesend. There boats with customs men at the oars were posted at the bow and stern of the ship and a Tide Surveyor and eight tidesmen went on board. At intervals the Tide Surveyor was supposed to hail the head and stern boats to see that all was well, and also possibly to re-assure himself that the boatmen were awake and not assisting in any secret landings.

These precautions did not entirely satisfy the Board of Customs, for at one time in 1778 they put forward a plan for the entire crew of the incoming ship to be replaced when she arrived off Deal. They wisely did not pursue this idea, because they probably realised that the

51

crew of a ship which had sailed half round the world would not take kindly to having to make the final sixty miles of their journey on the Dover coach.

Gravesend was the gateway to London as far as river traffic was concerned. Here tide-waiters and searchers went on board all vessels and remained there until the ship eventually discharged its cargo at one of the wharves in the Pool of London or one of the down-river quays, such as Deptford or Blackwall. Similarly, vessels leaving London were supposed to be cleared at Gravesend on their way out, but there was so much traffic on the river that it was difficult to be sure that this rule was obeyed· Daniel Defoe describes the scene in the 1720s·

"... When a merchant ship come down from London... as soon as they come among the ships that are riding in the road, the sentinel at the block-house, as they call it, on Gravesend side fires his musket, which is to tell the pilot he must bring to; if he comes on, as soon as the ship passes broad side with the block-house, the sentinel fires again, whicn is as much to say why don't you bring to? If he drives a little farther, he fires a third time, and the language of that is, bring to immediately, and let go your anchor, or we will make you..."

If the ship still fails to stop, the sentinel then signals to Tilbury Fort across the river from where heavy guns could be turned on her before she got to Lower Hope Reach, but, because of the amount of traffic on the river, it was almost always impossible to fire without risking damage to other vessels. Defoe describes how the gunners at Tilbury were powerless to stop a runaway ship·

"... a ship ventured to run off in spite of all these firings; and it being at first

52

shoot of the ebb, and when a great fleet of light colliers and other ships were under sail too. By that time, the ship escaping round the Hope Point, she was so hid among the other ships, that the gunners of the bastion hardly knew who to shoot at; upon which they manned out several boats with soldiers, in hopes to overtake her or make signals to some men of war at The Nore, to man their boats and stop her, but she laughed at them all; for as it blew a fresh gale of wind at south west, and the tide of ebb strong under her foot, she went three feet for their one..."

As the Thames twisted its way north and south after Gravesend, past Rainham and Greenwich and the Isle of Dogs, smuggling decreased in volume, but the number of people engaged in some form of smuggling probably increased; their activities confined to what one man or one boat could carry. There were fewer opportunities to land large cargoes unseen and no Master of a smuggling cutter was going to risk his ship and his liberty by sailing too far up river. The Admiralty had a form of semaphore signalling method in operation between London and The Nore, so anyone trying to make a run for it down river risked being trapped, although according to Defoe, the bold could dodge the Revenue or the Tilbury guns. However, the more organised criminals preferred to allow ships to bring legitimate cargoes up river and then set their ingenuity to straightforward stealing – to be described in Chapter Three.

Up river smugglers tended to be seamen or watermen making themselves some extra money, rather than organised gangs. This did not make the Revenue's task any easier, they found themselves working, not only on a river crowded with barges and colliers, but also having to patrol and pursue among the teeming population of the riverside; slithering and slipping in the muddy alleys and ditches from Blackfriars to Wapping, and finding themselves following their investigations some way from the river in places like Shoreditch, Seven Dials and even Oxford Street.

Oxford Street was part of the parish of Saint Ann, Soho. It was far from the busy shopping street it is today, but it did have some shops, one of which was a tobacconist run by Mr John Cooper. Mr Cooper was also a known receiver of smuggled tobacco and snuff. On two occasions within a few months he had a brush with the Revenue men. The first time was on 30 January, 1789. Three customs officers, Thomas Lewis, and his son, John, and Robert Whitaker, were watching the Cooper shop, having been informed that a quantity of run goods would be delivered. Lewis senior watched from one spot and his son and Officer Whitaker hovered close to the shop. Eventually a man was seen to enter the shop with a large sack. The two younger men followed him into the shop and found that there was 97 pounds of snuff in the sack for which there was no customs certificate. They seized the snuff and then the usual bribe was offered. Young John Lewis was taken on one side by Mr Cooper who pressed a half guinea in his hand, explaining that it was not worth their while seizing the snuff·

"...if they would leave it he would satisfy them, meaning as the deponents verily believe that he would give them money or other recompence to relinquish the same and not take it to the customs house..."

But young John, like a dutiful son, called his dad and passed on the half guinea:

"... and told him for what corrupt purpose it had been given him by the

54

defendant..."

Lewis senior informed the tobacconist that 'they were not officers of that stamp', whereupon Mr Cooper, who was clearly used to dealing with more amenable officers, offered to double the bribe, but failed to corrupt the Lewises.

The subsequent fine that Mr Cooper no doubt had to pay did not deter him from dabbling in smuggled goods, for on 7 September he was in trouble again, this time resorting to violence rather than bribery. Once again acting upon information received from some sort of 'mole' within Mr Cooper's small smuggling organisation, officers Thomas Wolfinton and Charles Bruce were watching the shop expecting smuggled goods to be taken out. Their informant had told them that the procedure was for someone to leave the shop with an empty box and walk a few yards to see if there were any Revenue men around waiting to stop and search him. If the coast was clear, he would return to the shop and load the box with tobacco. This is exactly what happened at nine o'clock on the September evening, the officer's deposition reads:

"... Thomas Thornley came out of the defendant Cooper's shop with a large box and several yards down the street and after looking about him for a small space of time returned back to the shop again and shut the door and these deponents further say that they immediately followed and placed themselves close to the window where they saw the defendants put seven or eight paper bags of manufactured tobacco into the said box..."

Thornley came out of the shop and walked 40 yards, then put the box on a cask outside a dye shop, presumably to rest. This was where the officers challenged him and he demanded to see their authority. While this was going on, Cooper, the smuggling tobacconist, came hurriedly upon the scene:

"... soon afterwards the said defendant Cooper came up without his hat and demanded of this deponent Charles Bruce to produce his deputation which he did and the said John Cooper then swore they should not take the box away and told the said defendant Thomas Thornley to assist him in opposing the officers and he accordingly did and assist when a scuffle ensued between them and a mob having soon assembled whom the defendants strongly excited to assist, the said tobacco was rescued and carried away in triumph by the defendants and other unknown and this deponent Charles Bruce for himself further saith that in the scuffle the said defendant John Cooper gave him a violent blow which knocked him down and he was trampled upon by the mob whereby his legs and other parts of his body were much bruised and hurt..."

This shows how quickly 'the mob' could be gathered to overcome the Revenue men who had no way of summoning assistance.

Charles Phillips, another Port of London customs officer, found himself under seige in a public house in Petticoat Lane in 1790. He was in White Lane, near Petticoat Lane in the parish of Christ Church, Spitalfields, when he saw a woman and two boys, the latter carrying bundles which, when he examined them, he discovered contained un-customed tobacco. He suspected that the woman was also carrying tobacco beneath her clothes, so he took her to a public house in Petticoat Lane, where he found 30 pounds of tobacco wrapped round her body. By this time a mob had assembled outside under the leadership of a local man, Abraham Abrahams, who made the customary suggestion that the

In the Kings Bench

Robert Harrison One of the officers of the customs
in the port of London maketh Oath That being on his
Station at Blackwall in the parish of Saint Dunstan —
Stebunheath otherwise Stepney in the County of ——
Middlesex on Friday the thirtyeth and Saturday the —
Thirty first Days of October last past and particularly —
on Monday the second day of Nov.ʳ Instant about two of
the Clock in the Afternoon this Dep.ᵗ together with William
Downes another Officer belonging to the customs seized
at Blackwall aforesaid several pieces of Chints and —
Muslins to a considerable Value concealed round the
Bodys of divers persons whose names are unknown to
this Deponent or the other Officer, and that before this Dep.ᵗ
could bring the said Goods away this Dep.ᵗ was abused and
violently obstructed by one John Haynes a ship Carpenter
at Blackwall and divers others unknown who Asaulted
this Dep.ᵗ in the execution of his duty and with great —
violence pushed this Dep.ᵗ from him and upon his attempting
to search him being Asisted with other persons then present
prevented him from his doing his duty.

Rob.ᵗ Harrison

officer should seize half the tobacco and let them off with the rest, but Officer Phillips refused.

The residents of Petticoat Lane were becoming so ugly out in the street that the proprietor of the public house had to close his shutters and bar the door. Officer Phillips was trapped in the building with the mob outside, but he found a man in the house 'who did not appear to be a smuggler or concerned in the riot, he charged him to assist in taking the seizure to the custom house', a task for which the innocent pub customer probably had little enthusiasm, for, as he left the house with some of the tobacco, Abraham Abrahams tried to slam the door shut to leave the customs officer inside and so separate Officer Phillips from his new assistant. Mr Phillips forced open the door and, brandishing his pistols, led the way towards the customs house on the riverside at Billingsgate by a devious route via Bishopsgate Street. All this time the mob, encouraged by Abrahams, was pushing and shouting and trying to 'rescue' the goods for which Abrahams promised them half a guinea. Halfway along Bishopsgate Street they stopped to swap loads, but here Phillips was pushed to the ground by the mob:

"... and the assistant not being able to protect the loose tobacco threw it on the ground and this deponent [Phillips] put his load upon it and defended the same with his pistols until the mob dispersed..."

There is no record of what happened to the unfortunate assistant after he threw the tobacco on the ground, he probably bolted while Officer Phillips was astride his seizure brandishing his pistols at the mob.

The smuggler Abrahams was obviously using women and children to carry his smuggled goods from the riverside, for only a few months later the intrepid Officer Phillips was acting upon information when he stopped two women in Bow suspecting them of carrying smuggled goods. Once again Abrahams appeared with another man, Michael Naton, and they proceeded to protect their investment:

"... he was collared and assaulted by the two defendants who swore he should not search them and a violent scuffle ensuing the two said defendants threw him down and dragged him across the road swearing with horrid imprecations they would cut his head open if he attempted to pursue them. And this deponent further saith that having no assistants with him and knowing the said defendant Abrahams to be a daring and desperate smuggler he was obliged to desist and suffer the women to carry off their loads..."

This sort of violence was very common against customs officers, for there was no police force to come to their aid. The parish constable was rarely around and, even then, was not always helpful, as Officer Robert Harrison found one day in August, 1767.

Officer Harrison found two men and a woman who had just come ashore at Blackwall Stairs; they had 12 china plates wrapped in a handkerchief, which he seized as being un-customed goods. The next day a Constable called on the officer with a warrant granted by Mr Justice Hodgson of Shadwell. Apparently the cheeky smugglers had sworn out a complaint against the officer and he was then taken off to prison for the night before appearing the next day in front of Justice Hodgson, who severely admonished the smugglers and released the officer.

Officers frequently found that, although

they had the laws of the land on their side, it was mob law that prevailed on the river and the quayside. James Cater was guarding 12 casks of sugar on Botolph Wharf, Billingsgate, when Henry Nantice and a gang of men came to collect them. Officer Cater would not release them without an order from the landing waiter. As the officer tried to stop the men taking the casks, they wedged his hand between a cask and a chain and hoisted him into the air where he was left hanging by his hand, which was 'very much cut and bruised'.

Apart from the times when customs officers were lucky or well informed, smugglers were fairly safe once they had managed to land their goods. The narrow cobbled streets with their overhanging buildings were unlit at night. The overcrowding and lack of building planning meant that many dwellings were only accessible by passing through other buildings. People lived and worked in cellars, some of them hollowed out beneath existing buildings, or timber lean-tos added to the back and sides of other timber shanties. The south bank, although chosen by the Bishops of Winchester for their palace, was a stinking, muddy collection of fishermen's and watermen's dwellings liberally sprinkled with taverns, brandy shops and whore houses. In 1756 a survey counted 1,500 butchers, 1,072 bakers, 5,975 alehouses and 8,650 brandyhouses in London. Once smuggled goods were swallowed up by the ant-hill of people with no respect for laws of a government which did not do much to improve their lot, then they were safe.

The smugglers and the Revenue were aware that the best place to try and prevent smuggling was on the narrow strip of water between the ship and the shore. Revenue officers in small boats patrolled the river by day and night, but their task was not easy. Foreign-going ships were mixed with hundreds of colliers plying between London and the north-east. There were also coasters and barges and many hundreds of watermen ferrying goods and passengers across and up and down the river, for the Thames was the most reliable way of travelling safely. Vessels were tied up to the quays three and four deep, as well as being anchored in mid-stream. Around all these craft there was a constant coming and going of small boats carrying crew, passengers, goods and provisions. The customs officer had to try to discover who was also carrying 'run goods'.

It was relatively easy to conceal small quantities of contraband in cargo or, as we have seen, under skirts, but when smugglers wanted to land a boat-load, they stood the high risk of being challenged by the tidewaiters. They had to select a moonless night, quietly load the boat without shouts or thumps, then silently slip the painter and let the river carry them downstream. When they were opposite a set of the many stairs leading from the waterside, the boat was guided ashore by the stern oar and quickly unloaded. The alternative to stealth was the employment of enough muscle to be able to out-row or out-fight the Revenue. Most smugglers did not try to escape when they were discovered because it was often possible to do a deal, either by the passing of a bribe or the handing over of part of the contraband so that the officers could claim their reward. When this failed, there was a fracas, often ending with the Revenue officers being second best. On many occasions they collected cuts and bruises and, nearly always, found they were outnumbered and therefore were not able to keep hold of their seizures.

61

James Kimbell was on duty in a customs wherry with another officer one October night in 1774, when they saw some men loading a boat tied up to the East Indiaman *Royal Henry* anchored at Deptford. As the boat cast off, the officers gave chase and soon caught up. They boarded the boat 'after some obstruction' and found 4 baskets of china jars and beakers. But one of the smugglers grabbed one of the baskets and threw it into the water. Kimbell leapt back into his boat and went after the china basket floating down river on the tide. This left his companion in the smugglers' boat with three of the smugglers who promptly took up their oars and began to row away with the unfortunate officer yelling for help. Kimbell abandoned the floating china basket and gave chase to the smugglers with their prisoner, to his credit eventually catching them. In the ensuing fight, another basket of china went overboard, but the officers finally seized the smugglers, the boat and the two remaining baskets of china. They took them to another ship lying nearby, the *Marquis of Rockingham* Tying the captured boat up to the stern of the *Marquis of Rockingham*, they managed to get their prisoners and the remaining booty on board and made secure. However, they left the smugglers' boat unguarded, so when they returned to the stern they found it had been untied and taken away.

Lack of personnel saved some other smugglers in Rotherhithe on a January night in 1784. A ship lying off Wapping Old Stairs was being watched and two officers were on the shore in East Lane, Rotherhithe. At 2 a.m. they saw a boat being rowed ashore by two men; it contained a number of bladders, which the officers estimated held about 40 to 50 gallons of rum. The officers waited for the boat to reach the riverbank and then set about arresting the two men. But they seem to have been rather incompetent in not realising that there would be someone on shore waiting for the smugglers.

William Polley rushed at them out of the darkness and, as he fought with them, the two men in the boat threw the bladders overboard and burst them with their oars, allowing the rum to be washed down river. William Polley was the only one captured and the deposition is marked £40, which was probably his fine.

Not all London's riverside smuggling was carried out by the lower orders. The merchants and bankers were not above making a profit from smuggling, but they usually employed more sophisticated methods – and made greater profits. In the tobacco importing trade, the practice of 'socking' was popular. This was simply unloading large quantities of tobacco into illegal warehouses before the ship reached its legal quay. For this they had to have the connivance of the tidewaiter who was on board.

Another smuggling method relying on the corrupt customs officer was the falsifying of weighing and recording goods as they were unloaded. The duty was computed on the entries in the land waiter's books. He could enter false weights or, if he was being checked by the land surveyor, he would use a false book. At the end of the day, the corrupt officer would get either a gratuity or a percentage of the 'profit', which he may have had to share with the weigher or other clerks.

Sometimes frauds began on the other side of the world. The packers in Virginia would pack a hogshead of good tobacco with tobacco stalks at both ends, so that the importer would only have to pay a lower duty on what looked like inferior merchandise.

Just as the amounts of duty had been changed and qualified in a confusing way over the years, so the procedure for checking and collecting the revenue had become a lumbering confusion. Those who were of a mind to could organise smuggling frauds which, provided they were not caught red handed, nearly always went undetected.

The hub of the revenue collection machine was the Long Room at the Customs House on the Thames side between Billingsgate and the Tower; Defoe describes it:

"... the Long Room is like an exchange every morning, and the crowd of people who appear there, and the business they do, is not to be explained by words, nothing of that kind in Europe is like it..."

The Long Room ran the length of the building, at one end was a raised platform on which sat the Customs Commissioners and other senior officers known as Bench Officers. The Commissioners and Collectors themselves rarely attended for the positions were a gift of the Crown to Dukes and Earls for services rendered. They just collected their fees and paid clerks and deputies to attend. Down each side of the Long Room were officers and clerks crowded shoulder to shoulder; they were allowed three feet of space to each man. These clerks issued permits, cockets, warrants, bills of entry, made up accounts, collected money, made hand-written copies in duplicate and triplicate with quill pen. All this to a background of multi-language shouting and talking from merchants, messengers, sea captains and other clerks. They had to go from desk to desk getting clearances, certificates and signatures and, of course, eventually paying the revenue due in cash, so the place was probably awash with money as well as a cosmo-

Long Room of Custom House

By permission of the Port of London Authority

politan babel of every nationality.

Because of the complexity of the procedure, most merchants relied upon the customs clerks to do the paper work for them, for which they paid a fee. This fee was a very profitable perk for the clerks and often amounted to several hundred pounds per year on top of their salary. It was so profitable for them that when one was promoted to become a bench officer, it was a considerable loss of earnings. This was overcome by taking a fee or percentage from the clerk replacing him, which led to an intricate pattern of patronage and favouritism that did not please the Commissioners: they wrote to the Duke of Newcastle on the subject:

"... these officers of the Revenue get more by these Clients (for that is the Long Room phrase) than by the Crown. This is notorious; and tis believed that when a promotion to the rank of bench officer one of these agents is disabled from acting as such (openly or directly) he retains a large share of the profits by recommending and turning over his clients to one of his clerks... the profits of some of these agents are supposed to amount to £700 to £800 a year... The Board of Customs therefore regret this practice, and keep a jealous eye upon it tho' tis out of their reach to suppress; and will no doubt continue as long as the various duties on the same goods remain unconsolidated..."

One of the loopholes for customs fraud by merchants was the 'drawback' system, which was eventually phased out towards the end of the century. Because of the Navigation Acts mentioned earlier, all goods, such as tobacco from America, came to England where a duty was paid when it landed. Any that was subsequently exported again was entitled to have a refund of the duty paid, this was known as 'drawback'.

To qualify for drawback there was an elaborate bureaucratic procedure. The exporter had to find the importer and obtain an oath that the tobacco was imported on a certain date which was checked in the Long Room by the clerk to the Controller Inwards and the Controller Outwards who made out a certificate. Then the importer had to swear that he had paid the duty on a certain date. If the goods had passed through a number of merchants' hands they each had to swear oaths that the goods were as stated. Eventually, the Collector Outwards granted a warrant and cocket for shipping on the back of which was listed the weight and contents of each hogshead. But all this circumlocution finally depended on the honesty and the diligence of the searcher who seldom checked each hogshead, he just weighed a few at random and assumed that the rest were correct. Even if they weighed the correct amount, they could be filled with stones or rubbish and could be thrown overboard as soon as the ship reached open water. But what usually happened was that the tobacco which was supposed to be on its way abroad was going to be re-landed somewhere else down river or at a small port, so that the merchant received his drawback and was still able to sell the tobacco in England.

Although the actual smuggling was carried out by the lower classes, boatmen, seamen, and riverside dwellers, it was not beyond even the most exalted of bankers to involve themselves in the organisation. There was an activity known as 'guinea smuggling', the illegal export of gold to Europe. As well as wearing English wool, Napoleon's troops were sometimes being paid with English gold. Napoleon himself is quoted as saying of his Peninsular campaign:

"... I did not receive money direct from Spain. I got bills from Vera Cruz, which certain agents sent by circuitous routes by Amsterdam, Hamburg and other places, to London, as I had no direct communication. The bills were discounted by merchants in London, to whom ten per cent. and sometimes a premium. was paid as their reward. Bills were then given by them upon different bankers in Europe, for the greater part of the amount, and the remainder in gold, which last was brought over to France by the smugglers. Even for equipping my last expedition after my return from Elba, a great part of the money was raised in London..."

It would be safe to say that smuggling touched most of the people living close to the river in the 18th century. If they were not taking part in running goods. they were often handling or storing them. Even the innocent and law-abiding were probably drinking smuggled tea or spirits.

Thieves on the Riverside

The rapid expansion of trade and the lack of enclosed docks combined with no adequate police force made the River a good hunting ground for 'light horsemen' and 'scuffle hunters'.

The 1700s were golden years for the waterside thieves. Like rats to a larder, they scurried between ship and shore with pockets bulging and boats loaded to the gunwales. Trade expanded faster than the dockside capacity; ships rich with loot swung at anchor for weeks while they waited for berths or discharged into lighters in mid-stream, thus offering more opportunities for pilfering.

Ships with everything from coal to exotic silks nudged each other on the tideway, while the quays were a confusion of heaped bales, sacks and barrels. The noise of boots, hooves and cartwheels rattled on the cobblestones as men and horses, the only source of energy, strove to load and unload the ships and barges. Boatmen shouting insults at each other pushed and shoved their wherries and peter boats into position beside the stairs and the anchored ships. The thieves could not know that this was to be the peak of Thameside lawlessness, as the 19th century began a police force was formed and the construction of enclosed docks began.

The tonnage of traffic on the Thames quadrupled during the century, most of the increase occuring in the latter half; 1797 13,444 ships carried 1,762,898 tons of merchandise up and down the Thames. The East India Company, whose first voyage was in 1600, was still a relatively modest concern in the 1690s, but during the 18th century it prospered to such an extent that it became a territorial power in Asia with its own standing army and a fleet of the largest British ships afloat. Other companies operating in the Mediterranean, the Baltic, and the Caribbean who began as adventurers gambling their fortunes had developed into sophisticated and profitable trading companies. Between 1780 and 1790 the value of imports to the port of London doubled from 6 to 12 million pounds.

Patrick Colquhoun, who was a campaigner for the setting up of the river police, gives figures which indicate the degree of crowding on the Thames. In the 4 miles of river from the Upper Pool of London to the Deptford chains there were moorings for 879 vessels, but there were often as many as 1,400 ships on that part of the river, together with attendant barges and hoys. There were up to 90 colliers unloading coal into some of the 2,193 barges employed in the coal trade. When full, the barges would frequently be moored on the river as floating 33 ton warehouses; these, added to the rafts of floating timber from the Baltic ships, increased the confusion and the navigation hazards.

The river was also a principal highway and was certainly the safest way for people to travel. There was a constant traffic of watermen propelling small boats between the stopping-off points. Every few hundred yards there were stairs or landing places: here passengers would pick their way between scavengers and mudlarks to be helped into bobbing boats. They could be seamen wanting to be carried to ships or smartly clad business men and messengers using the boat as a bus service. They could travel between dozens of points on the river for a few coppers, to Gravesend for 4/6d or across the river for a penny; the Watermen's Company licenced 40 river crossing places between Vauxhall and Limehouse and sternly warned travellers against 'pirate' ferry boats.

The only organised security working amidst this profusion of anchored and moving traffic on the river was the customs service. They found it difficult just to control smuggling, their officers were not able, or even willing, to prevent other crimes. Those who wanted to guard their cargoes and ships had to employ their own watchmen. They sometimes had to guard more than one vessel and were unlikely to be able to summon help if they caught thieves at work. The job was ill paid and thankless and usually attracted the elderly or the homeless, who found it wiser to sleep soundly or even take part in the robbery. There was very little regard for other people's property, nor was there much loyalty to employers, most of whom were anonymous figures who did not frequent the riverside. Once stolen goods reached the shore they were quickly disposed of and their loss probably not discovered for days, or never at all.

The social and geographical state of London in the 18th century made it fertile ground for criminals. The city had begun to grow rapidly in the 1600s; the population doubled between 1600 and 1650 and by 1800 had doubled again. In the 1700s the rich were abandoning the country mansions in Hackney, Clerkenwell, and Southwark for more fashionable areas to the west of the city. The artisans and tradesmen moved from the slum areas, like Wapping and

71

Stepney, to take their places, while the poor made their homes in the crowded riverside streets and alleys.

The size of the city and the opportunities offered by the expansion of trade, together with the beginnings of the Industrial Revolution, were a strong magnet for country people who were used to relying on the harvest or the patronage of the landowners for their livelihood. It was also an attractive place for the vagrants and criminals who could find shelter and a living much more easily in the crowded slums than under the eye of the parish constable in the country.

Building restrictions were imposed by several governments in order to restrict the growth of the city. Those who could afford them paid fines and bribes to overcome the restrictions, but the poor just sub-divided existing buildings; adding lean-to shanties and digging cellars, sometimes with disastrous results.

A 1703 map of Stepney to the scale of 150 yards to the inch shows the courts and yards to be so tightly packed that there is no space to name them except by numbers and a separate key; it also shows an open sewer running down Nightingale Lane. A haze of smoke hung over the fetid alleys and courtyards that stank of cooking, beer, and sewage. As late as 1770 a doctor recommending fresh air to combat typhus could only advise his patients to loiter on London or Blackfriars bridges.

At the end of the 17th century, the building restrictions began to ease, but by then the east London and riverside slums were well established as havens for the multitudes who made up the shifting workforce described by the Middlesex Justices as:

"... weavers and other manufact-urers and of seamen and such who relate to shipping and are very factious and poor.."

There were areas of London which were sanctuaries for criminals, who could once claim the protection of ancient religious orders. The legality of the sanctuaries was dissolved at the time of the reformation, but they were still areas to which few watchmen and constables chose to venture. There was an area known as The Sanctuary in Westminster, and another warren of thieves' dens and drinking houses known as Alsatia, located between Fleet Street and the river. The narrow streets and alleys were infested with pickpockets, footpads, and prostitutes, who had their own warning and sheltering system to protect criminals.

The watchmen and constables were the only agents of the law, for there was no recog-nised police force in any number until the early 19th century. In a system going back to the Statute of Winchester in 1285, local districts were responsible for their own policing. Con-stables and watchmen were appointed by the parish, they were badly paid and in some parishes the duty of the constable, who was a sort of executive policeman, was carried out by a rota of all able bodied men in the parish. This arrangement was adequate in more stable rural societies, but not in London. The job was a thankless one and those who could afford it paid others to do the duties, hence the quality of constables and watchmen sometimes suffered.

Around the middle of the 18th century, the lawlessness was disturbing many people, some of whom were advocating the formation of a professional police force. But this move was bitterly opposed by many who saw it as an infringement of freedom. Not least amongst these opponents were some of the magistrates and justices who saw their considerable powers in danger. They were paid fees for all the duties they performed and had an interest in perpetuating the haphazard law enforcement and need for litigation. They were known as 'trading justices' and some were bigger criminals than those in the dock, even resorting to blackmail and extortion on occasions.

The justices had the power to order the flogging, imprisonment, transportation or even hanging of felons. Because of the severity of the punishments laid down for offences, the justices' wide powers of mercy were courted by the accused and their defenders. The pardon was much more readily used in law enforcement legitimately, but was also mis-used by many of the 'trading justices'.

So the judiciary could not be relied upon for the fair administration of law in the 1750s. Things began to improve when Henry Fielding was appointed Metropolitan Magistrate at Bow Street, to be followed by his brother John. The Government paid them £200, later increased to £400 per annum from a secret fund, in order to bring their income up to that of the more commercial 'trading justices'. The Fieldings made attempts to form police squads, but mainly to combat highway robbery. There were also some private groupings of citizens who tried to form some sort of guard for their property. In 1749 there was a protest raised in the newspapers resulting in the public being invited to pay a subscription to a special fund raised at Lloyd's coffee house to form a special guard called Merchant's Constables. But these small bands of guards were intended to protect the property of those who paid them and no more. Similarly, the watchmen and constables had a duty only to their own parish. John Fielding, in his extracts from the penal laws laments at the state of the watch in Westminster:

"... The state of the watch in Westminster is notoriously bad and ineffectual, arising principally from the following causes: first the acts of Parliament make the power of the Commissioners parochial, this occasions too great a parsimony and causes confusion on fixing the watch at the borders of each parish; the pay of the watch man is much too little, their duty too hard, and they generally lodge out of the parish at a great distance... If the constables of the night were to be allowed something for that trouble, provided they executed that trust with fidelity by staying at their watchhouse the stated hours..."

Some of the watchmen were old, some lazy, and some blatantly dishonest. They had a stave, a lantern and possibly a rattle. If they were not asleep in their watchhouse or a door-way, they would call out the hours throughout the night, but be little use in deterring or catching criminals. Those who were diligent took great risks, as did William Ridley, who was a watchman at Blackfriars one December night in 1767.

There was a busy landingstage at Black-friars with a set of wide stairs leading down to the water. Large ships could not get beyond London Bridge, but lighters and small boats could, sometimes with difficulty, pass through the arches of the bridge to work up river. Blackfriars was a handy mooring place, but it was a rather dismal area for it was here that the Fleet River ran into the Thames. The Fleet was then known as the Fleet Ditch, because it had become so silted up with mud, effluent and the debris of its bankside residents. Swift described it:

"Sweepings from butchers' stalls. dung. guts. and blood.

Drown'd puppies. stinking sprats. all drenched in mud.

Dead cats. and turnip tops. come tumbling down the flood."

On the cold December night, a gang of drunken lightermen came ashore to the Last and Sugar Loaf, an inn near the Fleet. They complained that the beer they were drinking stank, but they drank it and asked for more. The proprietor said he was closing and asked them to leave:

"... I said it was past our hour, and desired them to go, they asked if they might have a glass of gin each; I said yes; they had a penny glass each; without provovation the prisoner [one of the lightermen on trial] swore and blasted his eyes, called me booger, and came and struck me with his fist; after that two others of them fell to beating Edward Crowther, a lodger in the house; then I expected murder, or some mischief; I ran to call the watch..."

The five lightermen were by then threatening and fighting anyone within reach. When they saw the proprietor had gone for the watch they ran out and apparently set off to meet the watchman halfway, the unfortunate Crowther, no doubt relieved that they had found another target, followed them with another customer:

"... I saw the bargemen run down the alley by the house corner, toward Fleet Ditch... when we came almost to the head of the steps, the men had secreted themselves under the houses by Fleet Ditch; they jumped out upon the watchmen; I immediately returned and saw no more of it, having been ill used enough before..."

Watchman William Ridley and a colleague were running towards the inn when they were set upon by the lightermen. Their lamps were smashed and Ridley's stave was taken from him and used to beat him over the head.

William Ridley died in St Bartholomew's Hospital two days later. Of the five lightermen, three were not caught; one, Daniel Afgood, was put on trial. Another of his companions gave evidence at the trial saying that he tried to pay for the beer and promised to return the next day. He also gave evidence that he saw his friend, Afgood, take the staff and strike the watchman, so he presumably escaped prosecution in return for giving evidence, as we will see later, not an uncommon practice. Daniel Afgood was later hanged.

The 18th century city riverside had not yet been walled in by office blocks, although the number of warehouses was increasing rapidly. The pattern of life for the waterside commun- ities was towards the river, rather than away from it. There were still many house-lined lanes and alleys leading down to the quays and stairs and other access points that played an important part in the lives of the local inhabitants. The river was a place of work, a means of transport, and a convenient dump for local rubbish – and the refuse of tanneries, mills, and dye houses.

The crowded alleys and tenements bor- dering the river housed a pool of workers who gained an erratic living from the Thames. Few people had permanent jobs on the quays, they relied on casual work which depended on the arrival of ships. Labourers who were hired by agents and supplied to ships to load and unload cargoes were known as lumpers.

The lumpers were the brawn of the river workers; those who worked the cargo in the holds of the ship were 'holders' and were often ex-seamen, while the others were 'deckers', who were required to lift and carry cargo to and from the quays and lighters. By the nature of their work, they needed to be men of more muscle than intellect; they were hard drinking characters, for the agents who hired them, or 'undertakers' as they were called, were usually also innkeepers. They preferred to recruit men who would return a large part of their earnings to the innkeeper by buying his ale; this was especially so in the coal trade.

Unloading the 500 or so colliers which plied between the Thames and the coal ports was a dirty, back-breaking job. As one can imagine, the men employed in the coal trade were not wilting flowers, they had to spend hours filling chauldrons by hand and carrying them to the lighters or the shore. With a dozen or so soot-blackened men shovelling coal in the hold of a collier, the only light and ventilation filtering through a pall of coal-dust from the open hatch above, one can understand the need for a constant supply of beer. The innkeepers supplied the men to the ships and the beer to the men, however, the men had little choice; the money for the beer was deducted from their earnings, whether they liked it or not

It was this small army of lumpers with access to the ships at anchor, that provided the class of thieves known as 'heavy horsemen'. The 'heavy horsemen' were those who stole by day from the lighters and ships. They took what they

78

could find and used ingenious methods of carrying stolen goods ashore. Their main plunder was, of course, the cargo; dishonest lumpers liked to work on ships carrying goods they could easily carry ashore on their person, for which purpose some would wear special clothing. In a treatise on the need for river police, Patrick Colquhoun writes:

"... Many of them were provided with an under dress, denominated a 'Jemmy', with pockets before and behind: also with long narrow bags or pouches, which, when filled, were lashed to their legs and thighs, and concealed under wide trousers --. By these means they were enabled to carry off sugars, coffee, cocoa, ginger, pimento, and every other article which could be obtained by pillage..."

In the jargon of the riverside, a frequently used expression is 'game ship' or 'game officer', this was a cant phrase to signify that a ship or individual officers were easy to steal from or corruptible. If the mate or captain of a ship was either open to bribery or was often absent, or the revenue officer on board was corrupt, word soon got around that it was a 'game ship'. There was intense competition among lumpers to work on these ships, some were so keen that they contracted to work for nothing, the contracting agent pocketing all the fees, and the lumpers helping themselves to the cargo.

The thieves among the lumpers were also greatly aided by by meanness of the ship owners who would not provide any food for them on board the ships, each time they went ashore to eat was an opportunity to carry off some booty.

It was easy to pilfer small quantities by opening the giant hogsheads, taking out a few pounds of sugar, tobacco or coffee, then resealing them, but stealing larger amounts needed the connivance of others. If there were 'game officers' on board, they could be paid to look the other way while goods were passed over the side to small boats. Useful people for this job were the bumboat operators who were like travelling salesmen of the river, trading in the goods needed by ships. They had a legitimate excuse to be plying between ships and the shore: they could easily carry extra cases, sacks and casks without attracting attention. Some of them were also prone to lifting any rigging or buoys that they could find. They became such a nuisance that the Bumboat Act was introduced in 1762, which tried to control their number and make them register themselves with the Trinity Corporation. The preamble to the Act reads:

"... certain boats commonly called bumboats, and other vessels, under the pretence of selling liquors of different sorts, and also, slops, tobacco, besoms, fruit, greens, gingerbread, and other such like wares... do frequently take occasion to cut, damage, and spoil the cordage, cables, buoys and buoy-ropes... and fraudulently carry away same... likewise to encourage seamen and labourers to dispose of such cordage... merchandise, materials and stores secretly and unlawfully..."

It was easier to pass an Act than to administer it, for it was 14 years after the passing of the statute before it was put into practice.

An invaluable aid to the 'heavy horsemen' was the cooper; many goods were shipped in barrels of various sizes from the 500 pound hogshead to the small half anker of spirit. The cooper had the skill to re-seal a broached barrel or induce a leak in a barrel or cask which had already been plundered, so that it could be stowed in the lighter with the leak downwards and appear to have been leaking into the hold.

One of the cooper's tasks was to draw off samples of goods from barrels for quality tests. For spirits he had a small pump, called a 'jigger'. The 'jigger' could also be used to draw off quantities of spirit that he could then put in a bladder and carry ashore in his tool bag. When he was drawing off samples of other goods, such as sugar, he was allowed to take two samples of $\frac{3}{4}$ lb each, but many of the casks were as much as 16 or 20 lbs underweight due to the trick of the cooper contriving excessive 'spillage'. The 'spillage' was that which was left over on the barrel after the cooper had taken the sample. This was swept up and put into a 'devil hogshead' which, when full, would be sold off as a perk for those in the warehouse.

The amount of stolen sugar available was big enough for certain public houses in Thames Street to be known as unofficial markets where grocers would go to buy cheap sugar. There were also some sugar merchants whose entire business existed on stolen raw sugar. West India merchants claimed that, towards the end of the century, they were losing £232,000 per year from pilfering. When they set up their own police force in 1798, angry coopers demanded more money because of their loss of earnings, and lightermen, who used to stay with their craft at the ship's side in the hope of perks, took to leaving them to be loaded and went ashore.

The demand for more money when the opportunities for dishonesty were curtailed is an indication of the extent to which pilfering had become a regular activity. All sorts of practices had become commonplace over the years and had been developed until they formed a trade within a trade. Certain officers on the ship were entitled to the 'sweepings', which were supposed to be the sweepings of the hold when the cargo had been discharged. Some also had what was known as 'private adventure', whereby they bought goods abroad, carried them home in the ship, and then sold them privately. It is easy to see how the 'sweepings' and the 'private adventure' could easily take in some of the official cargo; if the officer was challenged he could claim it was part of his legitimate perquisits. With this going on, it is not surprising that many of the lower orders were tempted to help themselves, although they usually had to take greater risks or use more ingenuity. A way to make sure that the watchman did not discover you stealing was to contrive to be the watchman yourself.

Ephraim McDone was a lumper, turned watchman, turned thief – albeit a rather inexpert thief. He was a lumper working on a ship unloading sugar moored at Wapping Old Stairs. He persuaded the Captain to let him serve as a night watchman on a half loaded lighter moored alongside. During the night he broke open a hogshead and stole 300 pounds of sugar, which he ferried to the southern bank in two or three boat trips. He took the sugar to the house of someone who was probably a receiver known to him, but there seemed to be little honour among these thieves, for at his trial the woman of the house, Anne Bowling, said:

"... He asked me if I wanted any sugar; my husband told him to bring it in, he would get someone to buy it (thinking to get the Custom House officers to take it)..."

To get to his own boat, McDone had to

cross the deck of another vessel moored alongside; while doing so he asked for a light for his candle. This seems a foolish thing to do in the middle of the night, especially as the man he asked was a customs officer:

"... I observed he was fresh with sugar over his hands and clothes; he went into his vessel, I thought he was about no good, presently I saw a boat go on shore. I heard him paddle backwards and forwards two or three times, I called my brother officers..."

Ship's officers went to the lighter about midnight and found that McDone was not there, he was making the last of his trips to the shore. In the lighter was a broken hogshead, a shovel and about 50 pounds of sugar in a lighterman's smock, tied by the sleeves to make a temporary sack. They waited for him to return:

"... He came all of a sweat, I took him and tied him, he got loose, and I catched him again, and put shackles on him..."

McDone's defence was as lame as his skill as a thief; he said, "I know no more of it than a child unborn." He was transported for seven years.

If the argot labels daytime thieves 'heavy horsemen', it is logical that there should be some 'light horsemen'. These were the night thieves, the real professionals who worked in gangs, usually with the aid or sponsorship of a receiver or 'copemen', as they were called. 'Light horsemen' were not just opportunists looking for what they could pick up, they were professional thieves who may well have had other occupations on the river, but whose main income was from stealing. Their methods were to use the darkness, the inadequacy or absence of watchmen, and their knowledge of the busy river and its banks. A well-organised gang of 'light horsemen' could empty a lighter in a night. With their knowledge of the tides and the flow of the river, they would cut it adrift and let it float quietly down river to a convenient spot before unloading. The less greedy, or less well organised, would employ a cooper to broach the hogsheads. They would then shovel some of the contents into what were called 'black strap bags'. these were specially-made bags to hold about 100 pounds of sugar, coffee or tobacco and be convenient for one man to carry; as their name implies, they were dyed black for use at night.

After taking 100 pounds or so from each hogshead, the cooper would re-seal them. These 'drum hosgheads', as they were called, would only be discovered when they were weighed and 20 or 30 guineas to a game officer could delay this for a day or so.

The driving force behind a gang of 'light horsemen' was usually the one who did not have to go out on the river, the copeman or receiver. While not taking the initial risk, he was nevertheless very important to the operation; he provided the finance to bribe officers and watchmen; he had premises wherein the stolen goods could be stored; and he had contacts with people who would buy large quantities. The receiver and his customers were probably outwardly upright and respected merchants, who ran only slight risks of discovery once the goods were in their warehouses, for the chances of identifying stolen raw materials after they left their marked packing was unlikely.

Some receivers were discovered and paid severe penalties. A Southwark tobacconist, William Escote, was a buyer of large quantities of stolen tobacco. He was eventually caught and brought to trial, largely on the evidence of one of his 'light horsemen' thieves named James Penprice, who was a self-confessed thief, who seemed to avoid justice by telling on his friends. He appeared in a number of cases in 1749 and 1750, giving evidence of how the accused and others, including himself, engaged on robberies on the Thames.

Penprice and another man, a pawnbroker named Joseph Watson, were members of a gang of thieves based in the Shadwell and Wapping areas of east London. Their activities show the atmosphere of treachery and self-interest in which the river thieves operated.

What Escote had done to upset Penprice and Watson we will never know, but he was brought to the Old Bailey in September, 1749, on a fairly minor charge of receiving 200 stolen sacks. From the evidence given for the prosecution it is possible that Penprice and Watson 'set him up', to use the modern term.

Penprice and Watson stole two bundles of sacks from a lighter at Bear Quay, a crime for which they never seem to have been charged. Some days later the two men were drinking with Escote and mentioned the sacks, saying that they did not know what to do with them as they had been 'advertised' – that is, a notice of their theft had been issued. This, in view of Penprice and Watson's other activities, seems an unlikely worry.

Penprice's evidence goes on:
"... Escote said 'can I see them?' 'Yes' said I 'I have got two of them here'. Watson went and fetched two. Escote looked at them. Said I 'I wish they were in the Thames again.' He asked how many there were of them.

Said I 'I have not told them. but in the advertisement there are two or three hundred.' Said the prisoner 'What shall I give for them?' Said I 'Give me what you will.' We said he should have them for a guinea..."

Escote's defence when confronted with Penprice and Watson was that Watson was a pawnbroker:

"... If I had bought them, no one is to be blamed for buying a cheap bargain of a pawnbroker..."

Then Penprice plunges in the knife by saying that:

"... he also buys stolen tobacco..."

What happened then is not recorded in the Old Bailey Sessions Papers, but it is known that the unfortunate Escote later stood trial for receiving over 40,000 pounds of stolen tobacco that he bought at sixpence per pound. He was sentenced to transportation for 14 years, ironically to the tobacco fields of Virginia.

During his imprisonment in Newgate he contracted gaol distemper and when the time came to embark with 139 other deportees from Blackfriars Stairs he had to be carried through the streets on a cart. The convict ship may have been marginally more congenial than Newgate, and Virginia's Rapahannock River more healthy, but there is no record of whether William Escote ever survived the journey.

The enterprising James Penprice certainly did survive, for at the same Old Bailey Sessions in 1749 where he was again as witness for the prosecution in a case involving the theft of ivory one January night from a lighter moored at Summers Quay.

A ship called *The Warren* brought in a cargo of ivory from Africa. The 193 'elephants' teeth', as the indictment calls them, were off loaded into a lighter skippered by a lighterman, Robert Davie, who approached a gang of thieves pointing out their value. There were five men involved, Davie, a friend of his, Richard Parker, and three others, Henry Faulkner and the pair from the Escote case, Watson and Penprice.

They took a long boat out in the early hours of a cold January morning and quietly drifted down river until they were alongside the lighter tied up at Summers Quay. There was a watchman on board and they sat shivering in the long boat for two hours waiting for him to go to sleep. By 5 a.m. they realised that he was a keen watchman and was not going to sleep and that soon the river would wake up and dawn would reveal them.

Davie, who was known to the watchman, agreed to go on board to invite him on shore for a drink of grog to keep out the cold. When Davie and the watchman were on the quay, the others were able to stand up in their boat, lean into the lighter and pull out the tusks. They had removed nine, weighing about 400 pounds, when the watchman spotted them and began running back to the lighter. They rowed hard for Hanover Hole on the south bank where a well-known receiver called John Root had a ware-house. They left the ivory at the warehouse and went to see Root at his home at Cole Stairs, Shadwell; by this time it was eight in the morning.

As the ivory was already at Root's premises, the thieves were not in a very good position for striking a bargain with him: he would not pay their price of 2/6d a pound. At one time during the haggling, Penprice and one of the others returned to the warehouse to weigh the ivory. At last they agreed on 1/6d a pound. Root gave them £20 and said he would pay the balance later. Davie, in his own defence later, claimed that he was acting on the instructions of the receiver, Root, so Root's withholding of some of the money that morning may well have been out of consideration for Davie, for he had been left behind with the watchman at Summers Quay when the others bolted.

The others made Root promise not to hand over the rest of the money unless they were all present; a promise that Root did not keep. Penprice, Watson and Faulkner later learned that the receiver had handed over the money to Davie and Parker at the Fox public house in Fox Lane, so they waylaid Davie·

"... we laid him down and hustled him and took it away from him..."

said Penprice in evidence. There was obviously some bad blood between Davie and Parker and the other three, for it was only Davie and Parker in the dock at the Old Bailey. Watson and Faulkner were described as 'still at large', while Penprice was giving evidence for the prosecution and was not charged. Eventually Parker was deported for 7 years, but Davie had his 'judgement respited' because he was claiming benefit of clergy – but it was found that he had escaped the hangman ten years previously by doing this, so he was finally hanged.

Penprice was to appear again in his role of the willing witness, who manages to get himself off and his ex-colleagues sent down. Five months after the ivory case, lighterman John Lighorn found himself charged with stealing 7 hundredweight of cotton a year previously. It appears that Lighorn became involved with a gang of river thieves. It is not surprising to learn that he stood alone in the dock, for his accomplices were the same gang as took the ivory – Robert Davie, who had by now been hanged, Joseph Watson and Henry Faulkner, (still 'at large'), and the canary of the waterside, James Penprice. Just to keep it cosy, their receiver was the ever-helpful John Root of Shadwell. Their method, according to Penprice, was similar to the previous occasion:

"... The Prisoner was in company with me, Joseph Watson, Henry Faulkner, and Robert Davie; we had a boat and went up the river to Summers Quay, we went on board a lighter and took out two bags of cotton; we carried one to John Root's house in Shadwell and the other to his house in Rotherhithe... the cotton was worth 18 to 19 pence per pound, we received 8 pence, we shared the money between us..."

John Lighorn was found guilty and branded on the hand.

Penprice appeared again later, but his activities seem to have degenerated into challenging people carrying parcles of stolen tobacco and seeing them fined ten pence. He may have run out of friends, either by frightening them off or by getting them put in gaol.

Unseemly Occupations

People who made unsavoury livings from the river. Crimps luring seamen to sign on for long voyages The Press scouring for the unwary. Innkeepers, whores, and tricksters relieving seamen and dockside workers of their pay. The pauper emigrants. Floating bawdy houses.

While the ten thousand or so Thames criminals were grafting away, there were many thousands of honest Thameside citizens who wanted nothing more than to quietly earn their living and feed their families. They were more independent than their rural counterparts, many of whom were still little more than serfs. This independence was frequently a freedom to starve, for there were periods when work was scarce, usually in times of peace when the army and navy were demobilised. To survive in these times of adversity, it was easy to reconcile the lowering of standards of behaviour towards a semi-criminal nature. The entrepot nature of London and other Thameside towns so increased and diversified the population as to provide opportunities for the enterprising and not-too-scrupulous to live off their fellow men. The Thameside spawned trades and professions between the extremes of absolute criminality and the placid law-abiding craftsman; their business, while not illegal, was often decidedly murky and called for people to be sharp and streetwise and not too interested in who suffered while they earned their living.

The early 18th century saw the burgeoning

of the distilling trade that the government encouraged without realising they were fostering something which was to become so pernicious that it threatened the whole structure of urban life, especially in London.

The country was producing too much grain for its own consumption, so Parliament, made up largely of landowners, saw the diversion of cereals into distilling as beneficial and encouraged it. Restrictions put on distillers by Charles I were relaxed in 1691 and, by 1714, anyone could set himself up as a distiller provided he paid a small fee to the Commissioners of Excise.

The inevitable result of this lack of control led to a proliferation of 'compound distillers'. These were often back-yard establishments, who acquired the raw spirit from the malt distillers, then added flavourings like fruit berries, aniseed or ginger, diluted it with water and re-distilled it. The result was a throat-burning spirit which was cheap and frequently lethal, not only to the customer, but sometimes to the distiller whose establishment was in constant danger of going up in flames.

Gin, brandy and other 'spiritous liquors' were on sale in all sorts of establishments. There was a law whereby alehouse and inn keepers, before they could be licenced by the Justices, had to undertake to provide quarters for soldiers if necessary, but those who could say that distilling and liquor sales were only part of some other business were exempt from quartering troops. This meant that retailers could set up a still or combine spirit sales with other things; so gin was sold by chandlers, tobacconists, barbers, street stalls and even tailors.

It was not until 1735 that effective action

was taken to control spirit drinking by greatly increased excise duties. The control was so effective that it became virtual prohibition with all the attendant evils. With no police force to control the drinking shops, illicit stills and gin shops could only be discovered by relying on informers who received £5 reward from the £100 fine – if they lived long enough to collect their reward.

In spite of a 1736 Act, the gin shops and the illegal drinking places survived on moonshine or smuggled liquor and even multiplied. A 1756 survey of London lists 207 inns, 47 taverns, and 8,650 brandy and gin shops. An average of one house in ten in London sold spirits, and in places near the riverside the average was one in five. It was here that the petty pilferers from the quays would gather to drink, plot and run up debts.

The licenced inn keepers were not above cashing in on the early 18th century assumption that the only amusement for Londoners was to get drunk. They were assisted in their task by the custom of using an alehouse as a 'house of call'. Houses of call were a sort of employment exchange, different trades went to certain inns to find work and be paid. Lumpers and coal heavers would have to attend a certain alehouse at which there was a 'pay table' set up on Saturday evening. As mentioned in an earlier chapter, the practice of the alehouse pay table worked especially to the disadvantage of the coal heavers, for the innkeeper was frequently also the undertaker or labour agent. The coal heaver, in order to get work, had to accept the conditions of the publican who took about 1/6d from his wage in commission. He sent on board the ship a large quantity of poor gin and porter which was also charged to the coal heavers whether they drank it or not. Anyone who complained was not given work or the 5/- per week loan to tide them over between ships.

Not all thieves were interested in stealing cargo; there was a ready market among junk dealers and ships chandlers for equipment stolen from ships. There were complaints of cordage, mooring tackle, boats, and sometimes even anchors being cut away from ships moored in the river. When a rudimentary river police was formed at the end of the century, an officer was put on board a West Indian ship lying in a repair yard in Wapping. It was to be re-sheathed with copper sheets. When the job had been done previously it needed 1,600 sheets of copper and half a ton of nails, but when it was done under the eye of a vigilant policeman, there were 113 sheets of copper and 336 pounds of nails left over.

A rich hunting ground for the thief were His Majesty's shipyards, where Royal Naval ships were built and repaired. These were at various places on the south side of the Thames between Deptford and Sheerness. In order to prevent the pilfering of naval tackle, the cordage and cables had a white thread running through them and the sails had a single blue thread woven into them, so that they could be recognised. When thieves stole any of these things they had to dye them. The most convenient way to dye large items was to find a friendly tanner and throw them into the tan pit, which turned them brick red and disguised the marker threads. This led to those who dealt in stolen naval stores becoming known as 'red sail yard dockers'.

The Royal Navy also had a problem when it brought prize ships up the Thames. Prize ships were enemy vessels captured at sea and sailed home to be sold or re-fitted for use by the navy. They were regarded as fair game for any light-fingered person, because their ownership was in limbo while their value was assessed. It had already been taken from its owners, so those thieves who had a conscience felt easier in that they were not stealing from a specific person or company; it was more akin to the spoils of war.

Petty stealing was made easier by the open access to the quay side and by the multitude of people who could contrive a legitimate purpose for hanging round the wharves and ships. Those who had a reason to visit ships at all hours, such as lightermen, coopers, and revenue officers always carried large bags or had commodious lockers on their boats. Even rat catchers devised tricks; once the traps were set, the rat catcher could then make frequent trips to a ship to check the traps, and not come away empty-handed. An indignant report of the time complains of the rat catchers:

"... It has been said that in some instance, they not only commit depradations themselves, but for the purpose of getting access to different ships, and to increase the demand for their professional labours, they have been accustomed to convey the rats alive from one ship to another, as a means of receiving payment for catching the same animals three or four times over..."

The labourers who worked on the quays and in the warehouses were nearly all employed on a casual basis. Their pay was low and erratic, when bad weather held up the ships they were sometimes out of work for weeks. They were known as 'scuffle hunters' or 'long apron men' because of the long leather or canvas aprons they wore. Magistrate Colquhoun called them the

94

scum of society and claimed that their long aprons were handy for quickly hiding whatever they stole. Their thieving was usually the grab it and run style of the opportunist, like John Lee, who foolishly waited too long before making his snatch and run. He was watching a man move a pile of 63 casks of butter from New Temple Stairs to a cart 200 yards away. There were nine casks left on the quay as the man made his last journey but one. Lee stole one of these casks and leapt into one of the watermen's boats waiting for passengers. "Row me to the other side", he said. "Where?", asked the boatman. "Anywhere," answered the agitated Lee, but the man left on the quay soon saw that one of the remaining nine casks was missing and bellowed for the boatman to return. At his trial, Lee said:

"... I was going home to the other side of the water, I do not know anything about the butter, no more than the man in the moon..."

The judge thought otherwise and had him transported for 7 years.

Although most of the thefts from the quays were of this petty nature, they were significant because there were so many opportunities and so many semi-vagrant casual workers who could pilfer in different ways and be tempted to 'lift', 'borrow', 'pluck' or 'take up' goods. The euphemisms of the time for stealing were symbolic in that they reflected the attitude of many people to riverside stealing; it was less like a criminal act than stealing from individuals, there was often a lot left after the thief had taken what he wanted, and the chances of discovery were slight.

The publican made sure that his pay

tables were not set up until late on Saturday night, so that the men could drink away a good part of their wage while waiting for it to arrive. The coal heavers' wives and sometimes their children would attend the alehouse on pay night, probably to make sure that at least some of the money was rescued for the housekeeping. This often meant that whole families soon acquired the taste for drink. The Middlesex Justices, in a report to Parliament in 1736, deploring the amount of drinking said:

"... Not only the vicious and immoral give in to this practice, but also those who are in other respects sober and regular; not only one person here and there in a family, but whole families, shamefully and constantly indulge themselves in this pernicious practice, fathers, masters, children as well as servants..."

The waterside alehouse on a Saturday night was a rather smelly, smokey den, sometimes literally so, for many of them were in unventilated cellars. Smoke drifted to hang across the upper part of the room and mixed its acrid smell with the ale and sweaty bodies. Honest and dishonest rubbed shoulders and many young men began to learn the tricks of the waterside while sitting in the alehouse with their father or mother.

There were complaints in the 1750s by coal heavers about the hold that publicans had over the supply of labour to the ships and the exploitation of casual labour. There was an Act passed in 1758 to break the hold the publicans had, but it did not work; in fact, the publicans even cornered the market in shovels so that they could charge for their use. It was to be almost a hundred years before the practice of paying out wages in pubs was finally ended.

The alehouses and gin shops were the only social gathering places of the riverside in the early 18th century; later there were coffee shops, but they were frequented by a slightly higher class. The alcohol drinking places remained important staging posts in the circulation of what little money there was. Apart from those who received their wages at the pub, there were seamen who had been paid off from voyages. They needed bed, booze and women, and the alehouse could usually supply all three.

Unmarried and widowed women without any skills or money were severely limited as to what they could do for a living; it was often a choice between prostitution or becoming a servant. The opportunities for reasonable domestic service were better in the country districts down river, but among the riverside slums of London, many women found that the only living was to frequent the alehouses, gin shops and 'twopenny houses', as the cheap lodging houses were called. There, for little more than the price of a drink or some food, they could ply the trade of a whore. If they were fortunate enough to meet a recently paid-off seaman or ship's officer, they could take the opportunity to rifle his pockets when he became drunk, but judging from the number who appeared in court, it was a risky business, for the penalties for thieving were severe, usually involving transportation for seven or fourteen years.

Women sometimes became involved in the crime of 'personation', whereby they presented themselves at the seaman's pay office at Greenwich and claimed to be the wife or mother of a sailor who had been killed at sea. They would then receive any back pay due to him. These tricks were usually carried out with the co-

97

operation of another seaman who was a shipmate of the dead man who could furnish the woman with the necessary information to make her impersonation plausible.

It was not unknown for women to visit ships while they were at anchor. The Royal Navy, especially in time of war, had many impressed men who could not be allowed as much freedom to go ashore as merchant seamen. Ships of the Fleet anchored at the Nore, off Sheerness, or up river at Woolwich, Deptford or any of the dockyard and repair anchorages, frequently played host to visiting women, both prostitutes and legitimate wives, who would be carried out to the ships by the bumboats or provision boats constantly plying between the ships and the shore. Some women were allowed to stay on board for several days at a time, although there seems to have been some discrimination between visiting wives and other women.

During the Nore Mutiny in 1797, the mutineers on board His Majesty's ship *Sandwich* demanded that First Lieutenant Phillip Justice be expelled from the ship because he removed the screens from around the hammocks of seamen whose wives were visiting their husbands between decks. It appears that the screens were not a privilege accorded to prostitutes for the mutineers claimed that Lieutenant Justice's behaviour resulted in:

"... our women exposed as the brutes in the field or common prostitutes..."

It is unlikely that too many common prostitutes visited the Fleet during the two months of the Mutiny, for, as you will read in the next chapter, one of the seamen's grievances was that they had not been paid for a year or

98

more. Those who did venture out into the mid-Thames were either very speculative women or were special friends of individual seamen, for they were not allowed to go ashore again, lest they carry intelligence back to the Admiralty officers at Sheerness.

At least one woman was sufficiently attached to her man as to try to escape with him when the Mutiny began to crumble. Ann Southerland from Edinburgh had joined H.M.S. *Tisiphone* in April, probably in Leith. She stayed on board with seaman George Ricketts throughout the Mutiny for almost three months, until she and Ricketts persuaded a boatman to take them to H.M.S. *Inflexible*, as *Tisiphone* was about to surrender. The mutineers on *Inflexible* had their own troubles and would not let them come aboard, so they eventually boarded H.M.S. *Belliqueux* where they collected another mutineer who wanted to escape. They all then boarded a small fishing smack and forced its Master, William Everett, to set sail for France. After slipping down the river in the night, past the guard boats, they were clear of the estuary and in the downs off the east Kent coast when fisherman Everett, under the pretext of getting directions from a passing lugger, managed to denounce his passengers and they were captured.

No doubt women visited ships at anchor in the upper reaches of the river; but most merchant seamen, after a long voyage, preferred to go ashore as soon as possible. They found the quay-side inns and brandy shops more attractive than the cramped quarters where they had been cooped for months.

For those who spent their lives on land,

however, the prospect of going on to the river for their entertainment was attractive. There were a few floating places of entertainment anchored on the Thames. Most of them involved drinking and gambling for the gentry, although many deteriorated into rather unsavoury places which only the gentry in search of debauchery would frequent.

One notorious example of a floating place of entertainment was a large houseboat, called *The Folly*, anchored on a bend of the river where Cleopatra's Needle now stands, almost opposite Somerset House. *The Folly* was a barge converted into a drinking and gambling night spot. It had an ornate superstructure which made it look like a castle with a turret at each corner. When it was opened in the mid–1600s, *The Folly* was a smart and expensive place for the upper classes who would arrive at the quayside in a cascade of crinolines and silk breeches and hire boatmen to row them out for an evening of sophisticated entertainment. There was dancing, drinking and gambling at the well-known 'Golden Gaming Table'. Thomas Brown, an 18th century chronicler who clearly did not approve of such places, described it in its heyday as:

"... a musical summer house for the entertainment of quality where they might meet and ogle one another..."

The ladies who visited *The Folly* were usually in the company of rich gambling gentlemen and, no doubt, practiced a more discrete immorality, for the place was respectable enough even in the 17th century for Samuel Pepys to record a visit there in his diary, but that was in 1688. By the early 18th century the place had deteriorated into a meeting place for the less respectable. The shocked Thomas Brown found that:

"... the ladies of the town, finding a convenient rendezvous for their purpose, dashed the female quality out of countenance and made them seek a more retired conveniency for their more amorous intrigues..."

In spite of Mr Brown's suspicions about the place, he rowed out to see for himself and found that he was being:

"... scrutinised by women both young and old of all sorts and sizes, some were dancing and tripping airily about the deck and some tattling to their beaux: but many of the company, including certain long sworded bullies were crowded into boxes in the saloon where they sat smoking and drinking burnt brandy, in short it was such a confused scene of folly, madness and debauchery that I left without drinking..."

It also seems to have been on the itinerary of the 18th century tourist, for one, Z. C. von Uffenback from Germany wrote:

"... All manner of wine and beer may be drunk there, but it sells prodigious dear, they play an organ and a violin as in gaming houses in Amsterdam. Innumberable harlots are to be found there and those who resort to them can take them over to Cupid's Garden..."

The 'Cupid's Garden' he refers to was Cuper's Gardens, a pleasure garden situated on the south bank of the Thames where the south side of Waterloo Bridge now stands. It was one of many pleasure gardens and tea gardens popular at the time; Vauxhall and Ranelagh were others close to the river. Most of the public gardens and tea gardens were on the fringes of the city in Southwark, Clerkenwell and Holborn.

The gardens were, on the whole, pleasant places where people could eat, drink and stroll about and enjoy entertainments, but a few acquired a bad reputation for attracting pickpockets and footpads, Cuper's Gardens was one of these latter. It was opened in 1691 by Boyden Cuper, a former gardener at Arundel House in the Strand. When he left Arundel House, the Howard family gave him some unwanted statuary from the gardens he once tended, which he installed in his own gardens, the broken arms and legs of some of them adding a touch of Grecian class to the walks and alcoves. The place soon began to thrive as a rendezvous for all classes, with entertainments as well as drinking and gambling amid the bowling greens and tree-shaded arbours. Patrons would arrive at the riverside quay, where there was a tavern called The Feathers, or they could stroll across the open countryside of Lambeth. But after a decade or so Cuper's Gardens began to decline.

In 1738 the gardens were taken over by a Fleet Street publican named Ephraim Evans, but he died two years later leaving his wife to manage them. Under the direction of Mrs Evans, known as 'The Widow', the gardens tried to improve its image. She did her best by not allowing servants in livery to frequent the place and advertising that watchmen were on guard to protect those going home across St George's Fields late at night. What is now a busy one way traffic system between Waterloo and the Elephant & Castle was then open fields with dangerous footpaths.

Mrs Evans also regularly advertised her Saturday night fireworks display – 'a miniature of the Royal Fireworks in Green Park' – for which she charged an extra shilling and promised

102

that 'great care will be taken to keep out persons of ill repute'. This promise was not kept for the same *General Advertiser* in which she announced her weekend fireworks in 1749 reported a raid on the gardens:

"... On Friday last upon information given to the Justices of Surrey that there kept at Cuper's Gardens several gaming tables by persons of bad character to which resorted a number of unwary gentlemen, apprentices, clerks, shopkeepers, journeymen, and gentlemen's servants together with the most notorious highwaymen, street robbers, housebreakers, and pickpockets. Sir William Richardson, the High Sheriff and the rest of the Justices met at the session, took to their assistance ten constables and a party of soldiers from the Tower, and with so much secrecy conducted the affair as to surprise them at their play, twenty four of whom were committed to the County Gaol where they may be seen by any person robbed. The Justices caused the tables to be entirely destroyed..."

This did not put either the gardens or the gaming tables out of business, for less than a year later there is another report in *Read's Weekly Journal.*

"... Last Saturday evening, a servant belonging to the gaming tables at Cuper's Gardens having some words with a person in the skittle ground struck out his eye with a stick..."

By this time Cuper's Gardens' reputation was beyond saviour and, at best, it was regarded as a rakish place 'where prudent young ladies should not be seen alone with gentlemen'. When, in 1752, an Act was passed requiring places of entertainment and dancing to be licenced, Cuper's Gardens failed to get a licence and was eventually closed after trying to survive as a tea garden.

It seems strange that apprentices are mentioned as patrons of what could be expensive places of entertainment, for those apprentices who were paid anything at all only received a tiny amount. Their reward was to be taught a trade and to get their keep; therefore many of them financed themselves by stealing, usually from their masters, while others teamed up with criminals and received a second apprenticeship, in crime.

The youthful herd instinct was just as prevalent then as now and many riots and ugly scenes were caused by gangs of apprentices bullying the populace, usually when under the influence of drink. One of the favourite group activities of riverside apprentices was to form cutter clubs. They would pool their resources and buy or hire a boat. On Sundays they would put on their best clothes, if they had any, and row up the Thames to Kew or Richmond. Sometimes as many as fifty boats would make their way up stream. Their crews would disembark and cause havoc among the small riverside towns and hamlets, somewhat like modern seaside invasions of today's Bank Holidays. In order to afford cutter clubs and drinking, many men would have to take to a fairly regular life of crime for which some suffered severe penalties.

Being caught by the law was not the only risk the Thameside apprentices had to run. The young men of the Essex, Kent and London riversides were more in danger of being caught by the press gang than by the constables. As apprentices, they were supposed to be immune from the press in their early years, but when the navy was desperate it did not ask too many questions and a strong young apprentice, especially one who was working for a waterman, carpenter, or even a tailor was a good catch for the navy.

The press gang was a constant danger to men of the Thameside. There were periods between wars when the navy did not need men, but as soon as the fleet was re-mustered to fight one of the frequent wars, there was a need for seamen to be found quickly. Sometimes 10,000 or more were required. Captains of war ships anchored at the Nore would send a lieutenant and a party of men out into the Essex or Kent towns to find a crew, or the Admiralty would set up a permanent 'Rendezvous'. The 'Rondy', as it was called, was a building part barracks, part recruiting office – for there were some who volunteered – and part prison.

An officer and a party of trusted seamen would install themselves in the Rendezvous, for which the Admiralty allowed them a maximum of a pound a week. There was a flag set up outside and, if any of the seamen had the ability, there would be pipes and drums to try to stir the imagination of potential recruits.

Although the activities of the press gang were covered by special warrants and their work was regarded as essential to the defence of the realm, impressment was an unsavoury business and often led to crime on somebody's part. The press gang personnel were frequently a pretty poor lot. The commanding officer had probably incurred the displeasure of his superiors, for this was not a task that bright, ambitious young officers saw as a stepping stone to commanding their own ship. It was more likely to be a form of punishment for officers who were sadistic or dishonest on board ship. The press crew also had

to be of a type who would not run away themselves and who would be willing to resort to
force on the frequent occasions when it was
needed. The result was that the press crew were
usually a bunch of near thugs who took pleasure
in their status as officially protected bullies.
They were also open to bribery and sometimes
took advantage of this opportunity to let anyone
go who could afford it.

The forcible recruiting of men for the
navy was a practice going back at least as far as
King John, but it was not until the 17th century
that it began to be used so frequently. As the
18th century progressed and the need for a large
navy increased, so the problem of finding men to
man the ships became more acute. The total
number of men in the navy in 1756 was 50,000;
in 1780 it was 92,000; and by the end of the
century 129,000 were needed. At first men were
threatened with up to two years' imprisonment
if they refused to serve, but by the time of
acute shortage in the 18th century, the idea of
imprisonment was quietly dropped, because a
man in prison was one less for the navy. It was
found more expedient to rely upon force to just
legally kidnap men and take them off. Those
whose friends were sufficiently interested were
sometimes able to use some influence to have
people released. John Wilkes was able to use his
connections in Parliament to secure the release
of Dr Johnson's negro servant who was taken one
night while he was walking near the riverside.
He was fortunate, for most men, once they were
locked up inside the Rondy, were lost to their
families and friends for several years. No time
was lost in getting the men on to a fleet tender
or guard boat and away to the Fleet. Those who
thought they had a good case for release became

'state the case men' in that their papers were marked, 'Let his case be stated', but when the unfortunate man's case was ready to be heard, he was likely to be on his way to the West Indies on a frigate.

The best way to escape the press was to either fight them off, run away, or get your friends to attack the Rendezvous, which frequently happened. A few were more fortunate. William Godfrey was sitting quietly at home in 1755, when the press gang burst in, knocked him down and 'dragged him through the streets with only one slipper on and thus put him aboard a King's ship in the river Thames'.

Mr Godfrey was shut in the hold with some others where there was 'a suffocating stench, the effects of which long endangered his life'.

Fortunately Mr Godfrey had some friends, for he was a cooper who had a 'protection' signed by the Lord Mayor who had him released within twelve hours.

Midshipman Robert Alsop and six others were later brought to trial at the Guildhall. It is not clear if they were on trial for their rough treatment of Mr Godfrey or because they chose a friend of the Lord Mayor, but they were themselves not without friends:

"... while the court was deliberating on the punishment to be inflicted upon them, some officers of the Government interceded, and prayed that they might not long be deprived of their services against the French; in consequence thereof, and on their knees sueing for mercy, backed by Mr Godfrey's generous forgiveness, they were only sentenced to ten days' imprisonment..."

Impressment, although looked upon as a

necessary evil, was not liked by the Thameside population. The grapevine would soon hum its warning when the press were in the neighbourhood. Seamen would stay out of sight or go into the country. They would discard their sea going slops and get into landman's clothes. The press gang would be on the look out for sailors or able bodied men who could be useful. They would move quickly through the alleys and streets, calling at taverns or setting up ambushes near the quayside, looking for men with the tell-tale gait and bandy legs of men who spent months stooping between the low decks of a man of war or merchant ship. Sometimes they would capture an innocent tailor, thinking he was a seaman, because tailors spent their days sitting cross-legged at their work and also became bandy.

Local Mayors and Justices were supposed to sanction press warrants and most of them did so without question, for it usually meant that the navy were sweeping up some of the vagabonds and thieves who haunted their district. The Lord Mayor of London did refuse an impressment warrant in 1776; he sent his own marshals out into the streets to round up all those who could not give a satisfactory account of themselves and had them delivered to the fleet tender lying in the Pool of London. His way of clearing the streets probably provided a rather motley bunch of potential seamen.

The Westminster Magistrates also ordered similar raids and gathered up large numbers of men under a 'privy search warrant':

"...the principal part of whom were persons who had not any visible means of livelihood..."

One of these searches on a night in November, 1776, resulted in a catch of one hundred and nine men, for which the Admiralty was asked to pay five shillings a head to the constables who delivered them. Even Lord Nelson himself was not above making forays ashore to procure the men he wanted; the *Kentish Gazette* reported in 1800 that he came ashore at Margate:

"... to procure from among the smugglers in the neighbourhood pilots who were particularly acquainted with the French coast..."

Most captains had to be content with a far lower standard than Nelson was looking for, even the lame were not immune. There was an Admiralty order in 1704 that all cooks and similar positions should be given to cripples and others showing lameness. Captain Baird of H.M.S. *Duke* wrote to the Admiralty from the Nore in 1759 complaining that his latest batch of recruits had men who suffered from:

"... fractured thigh bone, idiocy, strained back and sickly, a discharged soldier, gout and sixty years old, rupture, deaf and foolish, fits, lame, rheumatic and incontinent of urine..."

It appears he had an entire crew of potential cooks.

Those determined to escape the press knew that they had to do so before getting on board a ship and 'taking the King's shilling'. It appeared to be fair game to escape from the press party, but not to desert once on board a ship, so there were often pitched battles involving the press gang who sometimes had to retire to save their lives.

When Captain Brown of H.M.S. *Squirrel* anchored in Long Reach heard that there were good men to be found at Barking, he sent two lieutenants and 25 men out at nine o'clock on a July evening. They found plenty of good men and captured a few, but there were many more who came out of houses and taverns and set about the sailors who had to run for their lives. They released all the pressed men to make their flight easier and, just when they felt they were safe, they were ambushed as they straggled breathless between high banks. Their attackers were

"... a large concourse of Irish haymakers to the number of five hundred men at least, all armed with sabres and pitchforks and fell upon us and gave us a fair beating..."

Allowing for exaggeration to cover their embarrassment, it still shows that the press gang did not find it easy to capture useful strong men, especially when they were accompanied by friends.

A more crafty method of catching men was usually employed by the more experienced permanent press gang based on shore. They found it profitable to lay in wait at the quayside or on the river bank in hope of catching a seaman who was coming ashore to visit his woman or go to an alehouse. Then they could snatch him and have him locked up before his friends could be summoned.

One August evening in 1709 a seaman on board the galley *Martin* anchored at Limehouse Hole was sculling himself ashore alone. As his boat reached the bank the press gang pounced. He leapt from his boat and ran along the river bank, but they overtook him, knocked him down, and put him in their boat. Then things began to go wrong; obviously the chase had attracted the attention of people on the river bank and also the shipmates of the unfortunate sailor. Captain Astor, the press commander, relates in his report that:

"...This gathered a mob who pelted the boat and gang by throwing stones from the shore, and being pursued also by the galley's men who brought cutlasses in their boat with them to rescue their press'd man the gang were forced to betake themselves to a corn lighter where they might stand upon their defence..."

So the press gang were on board the lighter full of corn, while the galley's crew in another boat were trying to board. The fight between the press and the boarders appeared to be violent for suddenly:

"... the boat of a sudden oversett and some of the men therein were drowned, three of the press gang were forced likewise into the water, wherof 'tis said one is drowned and the other two in irons in New Prison..."

The remainder of the gang leaped into another wherry and managed to escape the mob. One can imagine that they rowed well down river away from the crowd on the bank before setting themselves ashore. The irony is that the man who was originally taken by the gang remained in the press boat tied to the other side of the lighter and was able to escape while the fight was going on.

The risks in getting men by shore-based press gangs and the poor quality of the 'catch', encouraged commanders of squadrons to use floating press gangs. Coastal vessels and home-ward bound merchantmen had to be on constant watch out for the press tenders patrolling the sea lanes. The press tender was a small armed vessel which had the authority to stop any British merchant ship and take off seamen for service in the navy. One of the most fruitful areas to patrol with the press tender was in the Thames estuary and the lower reaches of the river. Many a merchant seaman, after spending months or even years away from home, was taken by the navy when his ship was within sight of the shore. Instead of going home, he found himself on board a man of war and heading out across the Atlantic for a few more years at sea.

When the press tender came upon a likely merchantman, it would fire a shot across the ship's bows to make it heave to. Many captains failed to answer this shot and made a run for it; some were fast enough to get away, while others found that the next shot took away their rigging. When the press party came on board, they would order all hands to parade and then set about selecting who they wanted.

Some seamen had what were called 'protections' – a certificate saying they could not be pressed. These valuable 'protections' were issued to masters and mates, to sea fencibles who were supposed to be a sort of territorial reserve to fight off invasion, and to others who had managed to convince the Admiralty that they would not be of value to His Majesty in the navy.

The issuing of 'protections' was a racket that certain Admiralty clerks would indulge in for a guinea a time, while a certain Mr Bloucher of St Michael's Lane in London would produce one for you with a lifelike signature of either the Earl of Pembroke or Sandwich. The 'protections' were also issued to customs men, Trinity House, and some property owners. To prevent forgery, the 'protections' also bore a description of the bearer: woe betide any who grew or shaved off a beard after receiving their 'protection', for this was excuse enough for the press to take him.

The parade on the deck of the crew sometimes became farcical as seamen suddenly became lame, blind, or deaf. Others would have to be winkled out from hiding places in the hold, while a desperate few jumped overboard.

The press were aware that any ship from

which they took men still had to be able to sail into port, so they either took just a few or had a reserve crew of 'protected' men who, in return for their 'protections', had agreed to act as 'men in lieu'. The 'men in lieu' were put on board in place of the taken seamen so that the ship could be sailed to its destination.

The final indignity for a master who had been stopped and had his crew taken was the law that the press commander could charge the captain of each stopped ship six shillings and eightpence for each shot he had had to use to make the merchantman heave to. This payment was stopped in 1740, probably because it may have been the final straw to a master who saw his best men being pressed into service and he became violent.

There were other tricks for avoiding the press afloat. Knowing that his ship was going to be stopped and boarded in the Thames, a master would sometimes put into Harwich and exchange his crew for a collection of lame or 'protected' men who could not be taken by the press; others were allowed to slip ashore and the master would mark their names as having deserted or 'run'. A lament from Captain Bouler to the Admiralty in 1725 tells of a ship passing the Nore, where he had presumably boarded her in search of crew:

"...she was without a man belonging to her but the master, the passengers helping him to sail her. Her crew had all gone ashore by Harwich..."

But another message to the Admiralty in 1756 was more pleasing to their Lordships; a returning fleet of East Indiamen had been boarded between the North Foreland and the Nore and had yielded 230 men:

"... a parcel of as good fine fellows

as were ever pressed..." – the transfer of the men from the homeward bound East Indiaman with their sea boxes had taken all day.

Sometimes the entire ship's crew had a 'protection', because of a special cargo of government goods or perhaps the ship had undertaken a privateer contract. Many of these 'protections' expired on a certain date and a desperate press gang commander would shadow a ship or place men on board in order to be on hand when the 'protection' expired. Captain Bouler, the man who found the ship sailing without its crew, had another unfortunate failure when he boarded the sloop *Shandois* coming up the Thames from a trip to Holland one February day in 1725. He explains:

"... I put fifteen men on board her to secure her company until their protection was expired... but that night, in Longreach, the vessel being near the shore and almost calm, they hoisted the boat out to tow the sloop about and all the sloop's men, being eighteen in all, get into her and run ashore, bidding defience to my people's firing..."

Could it be that the press crew did not relish the hard work of towing the sloop into midstream, so they forced the sloop's crew to do the job and thereby handed the crew the opportunity to make a run for the Essex shore and never be seen again?

Another place for the vulture-like hovering of the press gang was Stansgate Creek on the Medway. It was a quarantine anchorage where ships suspected of carrying disease were made to anchor until it was certain that they were free of infection. Their clean bill of health meant that their 'protection' also ended and made them fair game for the press gang. In December, 1744, Admiral Rodney was fitting out a fleet at

114

Sheerness and the Nore, while there were a dozen ships from the Levant with over two hundred sailors on board awaiting quarantine clearance at Stangate Creek. So fifty men, under Lieutenant Seymour from H.M.S. *Royal Sovereign* set off on 15 December, seven days before the quarantine was due to be lifted, and rowed up and down the anchorage taunting the men with what would happen to them if they did not volunteer, assuring them that they would be shot 'like small birds' if they did not volunteer. By the 22nd, the end of the quarantine, the merchant seamen were reported to be in a state of 'mutinous insolence'. They had probably spent the previous week leaning over the rails of their ships telling the young navy lieutenant and his men what they thought of the prospect of going to war under Admiral Rodney.

There was no prospect of catching the men unaware after spending the previous seven days rowing up and down trying to get them to volunteer, so the navy mounted a series of boarding parties which, not surprisingly, were met by the sailors 'with presented arms'. Seymour sent for more help from the *Royal Sovereign* but while this was on its way the seamen broke open the lockers on board their own ships, took out all the firearms and took to the boats. One hundred got away 'after some smart firing on both sides'.

The customs men also had some brushes with the press gang. There is a King's Bench deposition from a customs officer about an incident in April, 1779, on a ship anchored at Bugsby's Hole off Greenwich. It was very slight, but it shows some of the uneasy relationships between the press gang and merchant seamen. The ship was the *Bugony* from Alicante, loaded with a cargo of raisins packed in frails, which were rush baskets. Customs officer Richard Cotton was on board, making sure that the raisins reached the warehouse intact.

The ship was boarded by an impressment party under the command of Midshipman John Jones. It is not clear if they were actually seeking recruits, but one can imagine that, even if it was a purely social call, the crew of the *Bugony* would be very anxious that Midshipman Jones and his party were not offended. There was a very real threat that some of them could have been carried off there and then for service in the fleet which was engaged at that time in the Mediterranean, the Baltic, the Channel and across the Atlantic. England was at war with France and Spain; the Baltic states were in an alliance of 'armed neutrality' against her; and she was about to lose her colonies in America; so it was no time to upset an impressment party.

Customs man Cotton was clearly a man who was conscientious and, because of his position, was not in danger of being pressed into the navy, so when the ship's boy offered a handful of raisins to one of the impressment party, Mr Cotton challenged them. He tried to make the boy return the raisins to the basket, Mr Jones became angry, challenged Mr Cotton to a fight and began slapping his face.

The Midshipman later appeared on deck carrying a knotted kerchief filled with raisins the ship's pilot had given him. Customs officer Cotton was still brave enough to challenge him and take away the raisins. It was then the turn of the Midshipman to show his rage, the deposition relates that the Midshipman turned on Mr Cotton and:

"... wanted to fight him and tore open his clothes and pushed his fist against his

116

face and trod upon his toes saying that he was not striking him, and upon this deponent [Cotton] telling him that he was not stationed on board the ship to fight but to prevent the cargo from being embezzled. Immediately the said defendant [the Midshipman] took this deponent by the breat of his coat and pushed him back upon the watercask and held him down for some time..."

The Midshipman then ordered his men to take the customs man to their boat, and indicated that he was about to be impressed into the navy; clearly a frightening event and a threat the impress crew frequently used to coerce frightened seamen and, no doubt, to induce the passing of bribes.

"... Accordingly two men collared him and dragged him to the gunnel of the ship..."
But the bullying Midshipman began to have second thoughts, probably realising that he would be making trouble for himself by trying to impress an officer of H.M.Customs and so he:

"... ordered his men to let him go which they accordingly did and the defendant then wanted this deponent to go down with him into the cabin to drink which he refused to do, whereupon the said defendant with his men got in their boat and rowed away, taking the handkerchief of raisins with them..."

There were other ways of recruiting seaman and soldiers not so overtly violent as the press gang, but were nevertheless only just within the law. There were certain people who carried on the Thameside occupation of crimping. A crimp was a sort of unscupulous recruiter who supplied men for the overseas armies of the East India Company and as crews for ships whose working conditions were even worse than normal. The crimp's clients paid him for each body delivered and did not ask too many questions as to how the men were recruited.

Crimps rarely had to resort to kidnapping. They haunted the brandy shops, twopenny houses and night cellars where paid-off seaman without homes or jobs would eventually gather. They would promise good terms of employment in India or rich pickings as privateers in the West Indies as the means of getting men to sign on for terms sometimes running into several years.

The crimp would also lend money to men they knew could not afford to repay it. When the man was firmly in debt, the friendly money-lender would turn crimp and offer the unfort- unate man the alternative of signing on to a ship or going to prison as a debtor. Most crimps found it useful to be lenders of money in some way, either by giving credit in an alehouse which they might own, or more usually by being dealers in seamens' wages and prize money. They would take advantage of the seaman's need for ready cash and 'buy' their anticipated share in prize money from captured enemy ships. If the man had any wages due to him, they were also willing to buy those wages by providing immed- iate money – of course at very favourable terms to themselves.

Patrick Colquhoun in his treatise on the river police is very scathing about crimps who batten on to seamen who he considered were rather naive and ripe for exploitation:

"... The known improvidence of the general run of seamen seems to require an additional degree of protection against that fraud and pillage and those gross abuses, to which their total ignorance of the means of protecting themselves, their peculiar situation, their habits in life, and their thoughtless disposition peculiarly expose them..."

It is difficult to imagine a hardened seaman being vulnerable to exploitation, but though their way of life was hard and physically demanding, they often spent months in a small wooden ship. They had no opportunities to become experienced in the tricks and sharp deals of shore based commerce. Their needs, upon reaching port, were mainly lodgings, food and drink, and women. But before reaching the shore they had to be sure that they were not going to be caught by the press gang and immediately put on board a man of war. The crimps were on hand to help them, but the price was often higher than it seemed; Colquhoun describes the procedure:

"... They were in the habit of going to Gravesend and the Nore, when fleets arrive and having provided boats they go aboard the ships for the purpose of bringing the men ashore, that they avoid the press. They charge them an exorbitant price for landing them with their chests and bedding and afterwards for con-cealment; by entertaining them and furnishing them with lodging, liquor and clothes, in many instances bringing women to them, the seamen get suddenly in debt. They are then arrested and when locked up and in distress, compelled to give will and power to the crimps to receive their wages, prize money, and everything belong-ing to them in case they should die. The crimps then procure the sailors another ship for which the captain pays them two guineas crimpage and a certain sum in addition is paid by the man. When sailors go upon their new voyage the crimp receives their wages, prize money, etc, and makes what use of their property as he pleases. Instances have been known where a seaman has brought home £30 to £40 and in a fortnight after he has been £14 to £15 in debt.

"It is also the practice of these miscreants besides charging 1/6d in the pound for the money advanced to furnish clothes and other necessities charging from 50 to 100% on the actual cost..."

When the crimps managed to sign the seamen up by either persuasion or blackmail, they often had to accomodate them for a period in a place where they could be secure and not run away. Many crimping houses had attics or cellars, sometimes equipped with chains. Other favourite places for crimps to keep their charges from wandering were what passed for hospitals of the day. This was one of the reasons for seamen to be so mistrustful of the medical profession, other reasons being the incompetence of most ship's doctors and the gruesome act-ivities involving body snatching from the gallows to be described in the next chapter.

One could see the point of the crimps wanting to protect their investment by making sure that the seamen did not run away, for sailors were not always the innocent parties in the jungle of supplying crews for ships. Some of them were able to take advantage of the Act passed in 1729 whereby three days could elapse before a seaman needed to sign articles which legally bound him to serve on the ship. Some sailors took their advance from the crimp, and possibly the master too, and then jumped ship before the three days were up. Others operated a more sophisticated fraud in collusion with the crimp who would supply them to the ship's master, take the fee, then organise their escape.

Some of the men recruited by the crimps were so low and wretched that they did not need to be tricked, they volunteered because the prospect of a soldier's life in India or that of a frozen deckhand in the Baltic trade was an

120

improvement for them. But where the skill and cunning of the crimp was frequently needed was to fill the crews of ships employed in the slave trade.

Most slave ships were based in Bristol or Liverpool, but now and then a discrete advertisement would appear offering strong negro boys for sale; a pub in Wapping was occasionally used as an auction room for slaves brought back to this country by enterprising captains.

The public of London did not experience much contact with slaving for the ships would leave the Thames on what was described as the triangular trade. They would be laden with goods for West Africa. When they reached the West African coast, they would off-load the cargo, exchanging it for slaves which the traders would have ready for sale or barter. The ship would then set sail for the West Indies or America, where the slaves would be sold and a cargo of sugar or cotton purchased. The ship, having left London with cargo for West Africa, would return some months later, with goods from the colonies of America, with little evidence of the highly profitable human cargo carried on the middle leg.

It soon became known on the Thameside if a ship was engaged in the slave trade and seamen avoided it, not necessarily because it was distasteful, although some professed revulsion of the traffic as early as 1700. A more cogent reason to shun slave ships was the very real fear of disease and injury. The slave ships very often had to spend several months trading and collecting slaves from the ports of West Africa. If they did not catch any of the tropical diseases, they could be in danger of injury during the storms or from rioting slaves.

Figures for the port of Liverpool in 1786

indicate the risks involved. Of the 3,170 men sailing in slavers 20.3% died and 34% deserted or were discharged, whereas the average slave deaths in a 1791 count were 8.75% Captains and surgeons had a reason to be more careful of the health of their slaves than their crew; if not more than 2% of their slave cargo died on a voyage, the master was entitled to a reward of £100 and the surgeon £50. Lost slaves meant lost money, but lost seamen only meant inconvenience in working the ship until the crimps could provide more.

Dealing in human beings was not confined entirely to the finding of crews for ships. There was a steady demand for white Christian labour in the American colonies. Many of the poor of the Thameside found themselves on board ships bound for America, some were volunteers looking for a better life and undertaking to redeem their passage money by working or becoming indentured servants. Few people knew what sort of life they were going to, some were cruelly duped and quite a few at the beginning of the 18th century were the victims of 'spiriters'.

Spiriters were dealers in people, usually children. They began to operate in the last quarter of the 17th century, after the Restoration. Their method was to kidnap, buy or otherwise procure people to emigrate to the colonies; some confessed to spiriting away over 500 in a year. The penalties for the few who were caught in this trade were very slight; an outcry against them and harsher punishments reduced their activities, but they did not disappear entirely, for a new profession emerged in the early 18th century whose legitimate title was that of 'Office Keeper'. They were supposed to be in business to legally enrol emigrants and 'redemtioners', but many of them were little

122

more than the old spiriters sheltering under the new title.

As late as 1775, seventeen-years-old Elizabeth Brickleband fell victim to a team of Office Keepers called Quirnforth and Dennison. Elizabeth was a simple girl who was not exactly kidnapped, but was duped in some way to going on board a brig called the *Nancy*, where she was locked up with 99 other redemtioners until the ship sailed for Baltimore. The girl's mother made vigorous attempts to trace her daughter, but was too late; by the time she found where she was, the ship had sailed. Quirnforth and Dennison, as a result of the mother's persistance, were eventually brought to trial as spiriters, but they only received sentences of one month and three months' imprisonment.

The more legitimate role of the Office Keepers was to recruit workers for the plantations by getting them to sign indentures for a number of years. The emigrants took the risk of not knowing the conditions they were going to find on arrival in America; some prospered, others were virtual prisoners working alongside criminals who had been deported from England.

Some emigrants indentured themselves to the master of a ship who then 'sold' them when they reached America or the West Indies. One captain was in the habit of visiting the Clerkenwell House of Correction where he would pay the fines of prostitutes and thieves if they would agree to 'sign on' with him for work in the colonies. As there seemed to be a steady flow of emigrants it was presumably as attractive a prospect as an English gaol or poorhouse. The inevitable trickery occurred when Office Keepers and Captains induced emigrants to sign on as 'redemtioners' or 'free willers'. The Captain agreed to take them across the Atlantic free of charge, provided that they found themselves a master who would pay their passage within a specified number of days after arrival. The fee for a trans-Atlantic crossing in 1770 was about £9, travelling in the hold of the ship. The unfortunate emigrants did not realise until they reached Virginia or Maryland that there was no chance of finding a master in this way; they were then in debt to the Captain, who was able to 'sell' them as virtual slaves. In fact, they were often worse off than the slaves, for slaves were the master's property for life, while the white servants had to be exploited as much as possible for the years they were indentured.

There seems to have been a steady flow of emigrants; in 1774 a total of 2,194 indentured servants and redemtioners left London for the colonies. There was probably an equal number of convicts whose only disadvantage was that they usually had to serve for longer periods; the work and living conditions they were going to were probably the same. Some of those who emigrated stayed and prospered, but few knew the hardships they were going to face when they signed parts of their lives away to glib Office Keepers in London.

Riots, Mobs & Mutiny

Injuries and death caused by striking coal heavers. The Penlez Riots. Sailors in fights to rescue the bodies of hanged colleagues from the surgeons. The Nore Mutiny

The relationship between master and man in the 18th century was based firmly upon a rigid class distinction, but there were stirrings of what we would now call industrial unrest, especially as the century went on. The downing of tools and the resort to mob protest have been here since man began, but in the 18th century it was used more as a strategy as well as in spontaneous indignation.

After the Treaty of Paris and the end of the Seven Years War in 1763, England enjoyed 13 years of peace. Trade flourished, particularly in the big towns. Urban society developed and expanded, supporting second and third generations of town dwellers who knew nothing of the self-supporting rural life. There was more dependence upon wages and prices and no space or incentive to provide food or service to be used or bartered. The greater independence of Parliament and of its members and the growth of administrators spawned agitators and pro-testers who frequently used violence and mob behaviour to make their point.

Many employers still looked after their workers with the stern paternalism of previous centuries, perpetuating a relationship in which

125

both master and servant knew his place and were each content with the situation. Those who disrupted this relationship were considered little more than criminals and harshly made to recognise that power was not yet in the hands of the people. However, protests were not unknown, especially among the Thameside community. Seamen demanded better conditions and saved their protests until their ships were in port, while the waterside workers realised that trade needed their labour to work the ships and to build them.

Political activity was spreading outside Parliament. Opportunists like John Wilkes were carrying their views on to the streets where the populace were impressed by their vague calls for liberty.

'Humble petitions' and addresses setting out cases were being presented to employers, the government, and whoever in the local administration or judiciary it was thought could help. These usually took the form of obsequiously worded pleas setting out a grievance and begging redress. Presumably some of these petitions were successful or resulted in some form of compromise. There were also many that were rejected and whose presenters were probably made to regret their 'disloyalty'.

To initiate a strike was not a step to be taken lightly. Any downing of tools, in order to be effective, usually had to be accompanied by a large force of strikers who were capable and willing to become a belligerent mob if necessary. The records which remain of strikes and civil disturbances involving Thameside people indicate that violence was frequent, but it seldom achieved any result other than broken heads, murder and subsequent hangings. When the size of the mob was sufficient, then it was inevitable

L P Boitard's engraving 'The imports of Great Britain from France'

that someone would throw things or wield a
stick. Benjamin Franklin, who was living in
London at that time, wrote to a friend in
America describing the East London scene:

"Mobs patrolling the streets at
noonday, some knocking all down that will not
roar for Wilkes and Liberty; courts of justice
afraid to give judgement against him; coal-
heavers and porters pulling down houses of coal
merchants that refuse to give them more wages;
sawyers destroying saw mills; sailors unrigging all
the outward bound ships and suffering none to
sail till merchants agree to raise their pay;
watermen destroying private boats and threatening bridges; soldiers firing among the mobs
killing men, women and children..."

Just as the protest methods of the
workers were sometimes crude and founded upon
mob violence, so the methods to overcome unrest
were likely to be somewhat unorthodox by
comparison to modern practices.

Woolwich was a riverside town which lived
very much upon the river business and was one
of the south Thames towns making some of its
living from shipbuilding and the manufacture and
supply of the goods and services needed by ships.
One of these services was the making of ropes
in the Admiralty rope yards; a business employing four or five hundred people in the 1750s.
The rope makers were not satisfied with their
conditions because the work was hard and the
rope lofts were damp and draughty. The final
straw that provoked a strike was their discovery
that the Admiralty was using a trick frequently
used to save money – taking on apprentices
instead of adult workers, thus saving a great
deal of money in wages.

The dockyard authority's answer to the
strike was unique; they sent in the press gang.

The ultimatum was 'you go back to work or we enlist you in the navy and you will be sent to sea'. This was a threat that their Lords of the Admiralty had probably used before to good effect, but the reply from the strikers was unexpected; they all volunteered for the navy!

Although there may have been an element of bluff on both sides, it is an indication of the poor conditions in the rope yards if the men felt they would be better off cramped between decks of a man of war in the Channel or the Atlantic. The Admiralty withdrew their threat of impressment and the rope yards went back to work. Of the reduction in the number of apprentices there is no record, so the workers probably thought better about a life in the King's navy.

There was frequent unrest in the south Thames shipyards. The shipwrights working for the Admiralty often complained that they were paid less than those working for private employers, a complaint still heard today. The reply to this plaint is also one given by modern governments, at least until recently; that government workers have the protection of continuous work and the prospect of a small pension.

A method of putting over views was the issue of a pamphlet stating the case of one side or the other. The Admiralty case published in 1775 replying to the demand for more money from the dockyard shipwrights is somewhat more outspoken than modern statements now issued by negotiators:

"... The impartial reader will judge whether they do not rather deserve punishment for their illegal combinations than redress for their pretended grievance, which now remains confined to a demand for more wages..."

The argument was over the shipwrights' complaint that they were paid two shillings per day, with an extra fourpence for tools, known as 'chips', while the private shipyards paid three shillings and sixpence. The only way the Admiralty men could earn such money was to be put on 'task work', that was a fixed price for a certain job, a move the Admiralty made to induce harder work when more ships were needed quickly. The shipwrights did not like 'task work':

"... this oppressive institution was unheard of until introduced into the King's yards, and if continued, cannot fail to destroy the health of the most hardy amongst them and must end in the ruin of every individual, and many families..."

The Admiralty's answer was that merchant shipyards paid high wages, but only by the day and they operated a strict no work – no pay policy, while:

"... in the King's yards the shipwright is paid winter and summer, wet and dry; in the merchant's his employment is uncertain, and in the bad weather he is rung off, and an abatement is made from his wages while he is absent; if hurt he receives no pay; when old or incapable of labour, he is left to the Parish..."

And so the mud slinging by issue of 'cases for' went on, but while these relatively law-abiding negotiations continued, others resorted to more violent methods. Whereas today's violent street demonstrations usually involve the protesters and the authorities, the 18th century protagonists were usually the protesters and the protested against. Any police presence was usually absent because the law was still represented by constables and watchmen who had no manpower and very little will to cope with large mobs. The only body of men available was the army who did not go looking for trouble involving the local population until the last minute, then they usually loosed off muskets from fixed positions.

An aspect of mob protest in the 18th century happily not evident today was the demolition of buildings. The less robust construction of some buildings meant that the mob could gather outside the boss's house and literally pull it down piece by piece. When the first sawmills were introduced in Shadwell and Rotherhithe, sawyers who were afraid they would lose work demolished the buildings and were only controlled by the intervention of a contingent of guardsmen from the Tower.

The most frequent source of labour unrest on the river was the coal trade. It was probably the largest single commodity business in terms of ships and men employed and was expanding steadily. The coal contractors claimed in 1730 that more than 1,000 ships were in use. It attracted enterprising merchants who were keen to profit from the demand and were no doubt not too concerned with the welfare of the labour force. They were also frequently at loggerheads with the watermen and lightermen over the operation of coal lighters.

Coal heaving, because it was dirty, back-breaking work, tended to employ many of the itinerant and immigrant workers who drifted towards London looking for jobs and settlement; most were Irish. Because of the nature of the employment, they needed to be tough and muscular; when they were in dispute with the coal undertakers, which was often, the result was inevitably violence and damage.

There were many incidents involving riverside coal heavers, the most violent being in the spring and summer of 1768. The coal heavers were demanding more money and less exploitation by the coal undertakers and merchants. In April they went on strike demanding, not only extra pay, but an Act of Parliament to change the regulations governing their employment.

The coal heavers assembled in Wapping and went in a noisy body from ship to ship 'encouraging' others to down shovels until work on the river coal wharves was at a standstill.

The men refused to re-register with their employers who began to recruit blackleg labour. The coal heavers gathered in large gangs and began to stick up handbills around Wapping and Shadwell explaining their case and condemning Alderman Beckford of Wapping for not helping them to get justice. The Alderman was the nearest to a villain they could find to vent their rage upon, but they were soon to find another. John Green, a coal merchant's deputy agent, was alleged to have sent one of his maids out to tear down the bills, so the strikers turned their rage on Mr Green. They lost no time in gathering, a hundred or more outside John Green's house at the bottom of New Gravel Lane, Shadwell.

Mr Green, who was a man of some authority on the coal wharves, heard the clatter of boots on the cobble stones outside his house. He went to the door where he saw a large crowd of men armed with cudgels, broomsticks and pieces of stone:

"... I asked them what they wanted with me; they cried, by Jesus, they would have my life if I offered to meddle with any of their bills; I said, I had not meddled with any, nor none that belonged to me; one of them cried, "By Jesus he shall have a bill put up at his window"; he took up a handful of dirt and put it upon the window and put the bill upon it. Another of them laid hold of my collar and drag'd me off the step of my door; another said, "Haul him into the river"; said another, "By

Jesus we will drown him." I got from them and retreated back into my house...."

The mob dispersed, but when Mr Green returned to the registration office at Billingsgate he was again threatened.

A few nights later John Green was awakened during the night by his sister-in-law who lived there. She was shouting:
"... "Mr Green, Mr Green, for God's sake we shall be murdered." This was about one o'clock in the morning. I jumped out of bed and ran into the next room where my arms were. I took and levelled one and said, "You rascals, if you do not be gone I will shoot you." They were driving at my doors and shutters, the noise was terrible, like a parcel of men working on a ship's bottom, I could compare it to nothing else. I fired among them, I believe I fired about fourteen times, and when I had not anything ready to fire I threw glass bottles upon them, they were at this for about a quarter of an hour, when they all dispersed...."

The following Wednesday the mob was again threatening to attack Mr Green's house. He sent his wife and children away and recruited a couple of friends to help him defend his home. As the mob, which he estimated to be four or five hundred, gathered outside:
"... threatening to broil and roast me and hang me over my signpost..."

He rushed from window to window, front and back, firing a brace of pistols and a musket; he claimed that they were loaded with powder only, but later in his evidence he says:
"... I imagine they would have broke in the house presently if I had not kept a warm fire upon them; I heard them call out several times, "I am shot, I am wounded"..."

133

It was probably Mr Green's guns that kept the balance between him and the attackers outside; at one time he crawled out on to the out-house roof at the back, in order to fire at them. But the beseigers managed to acquire a gun of some sort in the early morning. They were clearly short of ammunition, for a neighbour, giving evidence at the trial, described how the striker with the gun demanded the buttons from his coat and any pewter spoons which could be cut up to load the gun.

Eventually Mr Green began to run out of ammunition himself and decided that, because they were only after him, he would leave the house in order to save the others:

"... I took my blunderbuss over my arm, and my drawn hanger in my hand and went out of the back window upon the leads. I levelled the blunderbuss at them and said: 'You rascals be gone or I'll blow your brains out...'... I went over into Mr Mereton's shipyard, one of the shipwrights met me, just as I jumped, he said: 'Mr Green, follow me." He took me to a saw pit and shewed me a hole at the end where the sawyers used to put their things. He said: 'Go into that hole, you will be safe enough.' Said I: 'Don't drop a word but that I am gone over the wall.' I got in, he left me, there I lay until the guards came; I heard the mob search for me, some said he is gone one way, some another; they were got into the yard. I heard one of the shipwrights say 'He is gone over the wall and gone away by water'."

Seven men were eventually arrested for the attack on Mr Green's house; their defence was that:

"... they were there with the design of keeping the peace and preventing the escape of Green who had been guilty of murder by firing out of his window..."

They were found guilty and sentenced to death. But this was only one incident of many. On 10 May there was a mass meeting on Stepney Fields; a contemporary report decribes it:

"... their numbers considerably increased and they they repaired, with flags flying, drums beating and two violins playing before them, to Palace Yard where they were met by Sir John Fielding who persuaded them to part with their flag, to silence their drums and to discharge their fiddlers, and then, talking to their leaders prevailed upon them to meet some of their masters at his office in the afternoon, and accomodate their differences..."

The next day they met again in Stepney Fields and seemed to reach an agreement with at least some of their masters, but there was still unrest, with mobs parading and shouting "Wilkes and Liberty!"

The coal heavers were not the only ones demanding more money at that time. Journeymen tailors, seamen, and glass grinders were also agitating. So too were cloth workers, the weavers and cutters of Spitalfields were seething with dissatisfaction and, in the following year, were to be involved in ugly disturbances equal to the coal heavers.

On 11 May, 1768, thousands of sailors marched on Parliament, where they were addressed in Palace Yard 'by two gentlemen mounted on the roof of a hackney coach' and told that their petition would be considered in time, which seemed to satisfy them for they gave three cheers and dispersed. A further 2,000 marched to Wimbledon Common where there was a Royal Review of the Light Horse. The seamen managed to cause some disturbance to George III and presented a petition to him. Other seamen were more belligerent, they were boarding and unrigging any ship trying to leave the Thames and few ships managed to get down beyond Blackwall before they were boarded and their crews 'persuaded' to leave the vessels. Yet there seems to have been no co-operation between the striking coal heavers and the striking seamen. Later in May, the Lord Mayor of London gave instructions to the Justices of the City that they were to call out the guards from the Tower should there be any disturbances caused as a result of the seamen doing the jobs of striking coal heavers. This order was in response to a request from the coal merchants who were trying to break the coal heavers strike by using striking seamen as blacklegs.

There were many battles between coal heavers and seamen in May and June 1768. The *Annual Register* records the victorious coal heavers going off after one battle:

"... with colours flying, drums beating, and offering five guineas for each sailor's head. The ships below the bridge are obliged to keep a constant watch day and night crying "all is well"... coal heavers are grown a terror to the whole of Stepney and Wapping and commit the most shocking outrages..."

One of the most shocking was on the afternoon of 24 May, when seaman John Beattie was killed in a waterfront battle between seamen and coal heavers.

There were a number of colliers anchored together, Beattie's ship, the *Freelove* of Whitby, was among them; they were in midstream and the seamen had been unloading coal to the coal heavers on shore who gathered to shout and taunt. The day before they had gone on board one of the colliers, the

Thomas and Mary, and threatened to murder the seamen if they continued to work the cargo.

By two on the afternoon of the twenty-fourth, the situation was tense; according to one witness:

"... they came down outrageous with sticks and cutlasses hallooing for the sailors to come on shore and engage them... they stood about half an hour hallooing and knocking their sticks and cutlasses against the wall; at last they laid down their sticks and cutlasses and said they would not hurt them [the seamen]..."

The seamen were foolhardy, or brave, enough to come ashore in order to talk to the coal heavers. As they reached the shore and were climbing the steps they were met by the heavers. They all shook hands, but the discussion seems to have quickly deteriorated for a waterman who witnessed the scene described what happened:

"...One Peter Pratt, a sailor, came on shore, one of the coal heavers came and shoved a stick against his throat and said if he did not hold his tongue, by Jesus he would cut his head off. Then Pratt ran down the stairs again and took to the boat; one of the coal heavers came down with a cutlass in his hand and ran and struck him. As soon as they saw this all the coal heavers began striking; the coal heavers began to cut and knock about as fast as they could. Some that were in the boat were knocked overboard. Some of the coal heavers got into the boat and fell to cutting them. Some of the sailors jumped overboard, some lay on shore bleeding. The deceased John Beattie was knocked over the stern of the boat, and it being a flood tide he got upon a raft of timbers and one man got up after him and began to cut away as fast as he could..."

The seaman Beattie was heard to cry out:
"... for God's sake do not take my life, do not kill me..."

By this time there were about 20 coal heavers on the raft of timber brandishing sticks and cutlasses, while the unfortunate Beattie lay bleeding. The rest of the seamen managed to get into their boats or other boats and retreated under a hail of stones from the shore, but Beattie was taken to London Hospital with a cut across his skull from the temple to the back of the head, which had penetrated through and chipped off a piece of bone the size of a shilling, as the surgeon described it. He also had a broken nose and a deep cut on his shoulder, but did not die until twelve days later.

Nine men were ultimately put on trial for the murder, at least one of whom was previously engaged in the siege of Mr Green's house.

By July, the coal heavers were so belligerent that it was unsafe for anyone to be out at night in Wapping and Shadwell. On the sixteenth, the nine men were tried for the murder of seaman Beattie, two of them being sentenced to be hanged. This may have prompted even more violence, for the *Westminster Journal* reported more disturbances in Back Lane, Lower Wapping, and Shadwell. A master wharfinger, already wounded from an attack two months earlier, was set upon near Farthing Fields, Wapping. A man on crutches was attacked and suffered a broken arm. A 'gentleman' was left almost dead in the fields adjoining Back Lane, Radcliff, after being assaulted by three coal heavers. Finally, troops were once more called out.

The trial of the Shadwell murderers and the frequent use of troops began to demoralise the heavers, who either re-registered or tried to

escape the military by making their ways northward to Liverpool and possibly a return to
Ireland. Some were captured on the journey
north by a platoon of light horse near Coventry
and returned in chains to New Prison,
Clerkenwell.

The final demoralisation was the trial on
26 July of three men implicated in the attack on
Mr Green's house in Shadwell, together with two
others for a similar attempt to demolish the
home of a victualler in Radcliff. They were
sentenced to be hanged and, as justice was swift
in those days, they were taken next day to Sun
Tavern Fields, Shadwell, for execution in the
locality of their crime, the *Annual Register* describes the scene:

"...taken in three carts to Sun
Tavern Fields, Shadwell. They were all remark-
ably stout, well made men and much excited the
pity of an incredible number of spectators who
were assembled in the streets as well as at all
the windows in the places through which they
passed. They were preceded by two sheriffs and
a prodigious number of peace officers. A guard
of three hundred soldiers did duty about
Wapping, Shadwell, etc., but there was no need
for their assistance, not being the least attempt
to rescue the malefactors..."

The reference to the possibility of a
rescue was an indication that such desperate
measures were not unknown. Whenever a condemned man was likely to have a number of
supporters, authority was very nervous about a
last minute skirmish to rescue the prisoner from
the gallows. For decades, seamen had been
notorious for banding together to thwart those
who they claimed were exploiting them. They
were particularly resentful of the surgeons
whose representatives would haunt Execution

139

Dock, Wapping, or Tyburn to try to snatch the bodies of those executed. As a large number of the condemned were seamen or 'of sea going type', sailors were many times joined in battle beneath the gallows.

Another factor that did not endear the surgeons to the average seaman was that a seaman's experience of the medical profession was probably confined to the treatment he received at the hands of a ship's surgeon, many of who were doctors who went to sea because they were unable to get employment ashore. They were little more than crude butchers, frequently drunk.

The expansion of the teaching and practice of medicine meant that there was a demand for bodies on which aspiring surgeons could be instructed. The Royal College of Physicians and the Company of Barber-Surgeons were allowed by an Act of Elizabeth I to have ten bodies per year from those 'condemned to death within London, Middlesex, or Surrey for anatomical dissection', but there were many private medical schools competing in the grue-some market. As a form of more aggravated death sentence, the justice would sometimes specify that the felon's body should be turned over to the surgeons for dissection. This, to many, was a fate they feared as much as execution, sometimes more so. Many last wishes to the Ordinary of Newgate were that the poor wretch could be protected from the surgeons' beadles and laid to rest in a Christian burial. Samuel Richardson described the scene at Tyburn:

"...as soon as the creatures were half dead, I was much suprised, before such a number of peace officers, to see the populace fall to haling and pulling the carcases with such

earnestness as to occasion several warm en-
counters, and broken heads. These I was told
were friends of the persons executed, or some
persons sent by private surgeons to obtain bodies
for dissection. The contests between these were
fierce and bloody, and frightful to look at; so
that I made the best of my way out of the
crowd."

Seamen, when they became determinedly
aggressive, seemed to have been a force to be
reckoned with; a newspaper of December, 1738,
tells of the scene when James Buchanan was
hanged for killing a fellow seaman in the East
Indies: he was taken from Newgate to Execution
Dock, Wapping:

"... as soon as he was tied up
some sailors got on the scaffold and endeav-
oured to cut him down, on which a scuffle
ensued between them and the officers, but many
other sailors coming to the assistance of those
who first made the attempt, he was cut down
in less than five minutes after he was hung up,
and his body carried off in a boat with loud
acclamations of joy accompanied by at least
three score sailors..."

Seamen banded together in 1763 during
what seemed to be an official purge against
prostitution. Peace officers raided some 'houses
of ill fame', as the records call them, in the
Tower Hill area and several women and sailors
were arrested. When they were taken before the
Justices the next day, there were large mobs of
sailors gathering. It was feared that they would
try to rescue the sailors and women, so troops
were called out from the Tower garrison. The
mobs dispersed, but in the afternoon, as the
prisoners and an escort of a sergeant and twelve
men was passing through Chiswell Street, they
were ambushed by the sailors who released their

141

comrades and the women and wounded two soldiers. When a similar thing happened a few months later, the army were more ready and killed four seamen in the fight.

A decade or so earlier, seamen were instrumental in what became known as the Penlez Riots, after an unfortunate wig maker named Bosavern Penlez, himself only marginally involved in the disturbances, but whose conviction and subsequent execution became a *cause celèbre* taking in Henry Fielding, who was at that time Chairman of the Westminster Quarter Sessions.

On the evening of 30 July, 1749, a seaman from the man of war *Grafton* claimed he was robbed of two Portuguese moidores in a bawdy house in the Strand called The Crown. The next day, the seaman returned with a large contingent of his shipmates and proceded, in the previously described 18th century manner, to dismantle the building. They threw furniture from the windows and made it into a large bonfire in the middle of the Strand, while they 'suffered no injury to be done to the damsels'. Troops were called out, but they just kept guard on the smouldering remains of the bonfire until the seamen dispersed. The next night, a Sunday, a mob of 400 or more marched down the Strand ringing hand bells and began to attack other bawdy houses. The Bunch of Grapes was burned down, then they turned their attention to The Star in Devereaux Court.

The next day the mob again assembled and the targets included, apart from bawdy houses, the Old Bailey Court where one seaman was rescued from gaol. Henry Fielding was under seige in this office and had to send to the Secretary for War for troops to be called out.

142

During the course of the riots several men were arrested, including the man Penlez who was found in Bell Yard with some women's lace garments stolen from the Star stuffed under his shirt.

Eventually Penlez was the only one of those detained to be sentenced to death. Justice Fielding was subjected to criticism because, although he had previously pronounced against bawdy houses, there was a suspicion that he and other justices took bribes from inn and bawdy house keepers and this was why he called out troops to suppress the riots. Fielding wrote a somewhat flowery justification of his actions, claiming that the seamen were intent upon stealing.

On the day of the hanging, Penlez was to be 'turned off' together with 14 others. Crowds gathered at the Old Bailey and it was feared that they would try to rescue him, especially as a large part of the crowd were sailors who had successfully attacked Bow Street a few months earlier. The journey of the six tumbrils from Newgate to Tyburn was escorted by constable and sheriffs of the divisions of London through which the condemned were to be paraded, plus as many marshals, attendants and servants as could be collected, making 300 in all. Theodore Janssen, Sheriff of London, refrained from adding a party of foot guards to the escort in order not to provoke more trouble. There was a double ring of mounted peace officers round the gallows at Tyburn and, although there was a large body of seamen armed with sticks and cutlasses, they were persuaded not to attack the gallows after Sheriff Janssen had promised to have the bodies delivered to relatives and not to the surgeons.

Although rioting and mob protest was

143

most frequent on shore, the Thames event which
probably had the most effect on the nation, and
certainly caused a great deal of trouble to the
government of the day, was the naval mutiny at
the Nore in the summer of 1797.

The Great Nore and the Little Nore were
large anchorages in the Thames estuary off the
mouth of the Medway. Here, ships of the North
Sea and the Channel fleets gathered to be
assigned stations and to be re-equipped from
the dockyards at Chatham. Along with Spithead.
off Portsmouth, the Nore was one of the great
gathering places of British naval strength.

Below deck, conditions in the navy were
appalling. Men had to live for months or years
in cramped, wet conditions.They had to eat and
sleep between dark, unheated decks stinking of
tar, bilge and unwashed bodies. There was no
room even to stand upright. Discipline was
harsh, with floggings and executions as the
principal inducements to conform. Shore leave,
even after very long voyages, was hardly ever
granted for fear of desertion. The officers had
the power of life and death over the men, who
saw their superiors enjoying the best of food
and wine, while the seamen were given water
alive with creatures and green with algae. The
salt pork and beef was nut-hard from its
months in the brine barrel. The bread was
described by one man thus:

"You have to watch very narrowly
the bread you eat, or the inhabitant animalcules
will walk away, house and all on their backs..."

The regulations called for a good ration
of beef, pork, and bacon, together with beer
and wine, cheese, bread and biscuit. Few sailors
saw much of this ration. As the fleet expanded,
so the Admiralty became more lax with vict-
ualling payments. Officers and pursers conspired

with chandlers on shore to defraud at every turn. To become a purser one had to pay a substantial sum of money to the man whose place you were taking, because it was a pathway to prosperity. Poor, adulterated flour was issued instead of meat, materials like wax, glue and waste fats were added to cheese to expand its bulk.

As if bad conditions were not enough, the men were not being paid regularly; some claimed to be owed pay and prize money going back two or three years. In 1796, the Admiralty estimated that arrears of pay owing to seamen amounted to 1.4 million pounds.

It seems incredible that the government could allow these conditions in view of the importance of the navy to Britain at that time. The French were gathering at their Channel ports ready to invade: they had already made one abortive attempt in Ireland. The British fleet now numbered 100,000 men, some of whom were spending many cold, uncomfortable months blockading Brest, the Texel, and Cadiz; they were Britain's only real defence against invasion.

The conditions to provoke a mutiny clearly prevailed. Additionally, there was a general air of disenchantment, if not revolution, in the urban populations on shore. The French Revolution, which had begun nine years earlier, was seen by many as a significant and welcome sign of the new liberty for the lower classes. Civic disorder was happening more often. There were also less violent and more intellectual movements of reform, like the London Corresponding Society, whose open-air meetings attracted many thousands of people interested in their aims of Parliamentary reform. The printing presses were turning out tracts and pamphlets

145

urging radical changes and challenging the Whig land-owning government. Tom Paine's ideas on reform and the apparent success of the American revolutionaries were having an effect.

It was in this general atmosphere of discontent that the patience of the sailors snapped. The unrest began at Spithead, where the successful outcome of the mutiny there encouraged the Nore mutineers to demand more and so eventually find themselves facing the hangman.

Spithead was the anchorage of the Channel Fleet; it was an area of water between Portsmouth and the Isle of Wight. Squadrons of ships were going to and fro to the blockade off Brest, but while at anchor at Spithead, seamen were not allowed to go ashore. They saw their officers going off to Portsmouth and London, while others remained to rule by the lash and the rope's end.

The seamen had learned some of the tactical lessons of mob protest; they needed to stick together in order not to be picked off ship by ship and they needed to fudge the dangerous practice of having one man singled out as a leader. At a secret meeting on board H.M.S. *Queen Charlotte* on the morning of 27 February, 1797, a 'humble petition' was composed which obsequiously asked their Lordships of the Admiralty for an increase in pay in line with that already awarded to the army almost two years before.

Copies of this 300 word petition were secretly distributed to other ships of the Fleet, who each copied them out again. The petition confined itself to pay, but some of the ships' companies added their own riders on other grievances.

Most of the petitions were addressed to

Admiral Earl Howe, the ageing Admiral in command of the victorious British fleet at the battle known as The Glorious First of June in 1794. He was known as 'Black Dick' Howe and was a well-respected commander of the Fleet at Spithead and had been, for a brief period, a First Lord of the Admiralty. At the time of the petitions Howe was ill with gout and his Deputy, Lord Bridport, did nothing about them. After more than a month, the seamen began to refuse to sail their ships. At Easter, 1797, the mutineers' rallying cries in the form of three cheers could be heard across the fleet anchorage at Spithead. Red flags were hoisted, officers locked in their cabins and ominous yard ropes rigged. Yard ropes were lengths of rope with a noose at one end, while the other was run through a pulley on the yard arm ready for an execution. No one was hanged, but hesitant mutineers and officers contemplating heroics seem to have got the message.

At last, Howe was recalled and deputed by the government to meet the men and he eventually negotiated a settlement with them for more pay. The wages of an able seaman and petty officers were increased by five shillings and sixpence and ordinary seamen four and sixpence, while impressed landsmen received an extra three and sixpence per month. There were promises of other improvements and some officers were removed from ships, including one Admiral, but the removal of officers was never admitted in writing, a cunning move which was to cause trouble for the Nore mutineers later.

Another fatal event for the Nore men was the sudden delay in the signing of the agreement at Spithead. Encouraged by the success of their mutiny so far, the strikers at Spithead demanded that there should be an Act

147

of Parliament signed by the King guaranteeing their increase and, until they could see that document, they would not return to their duties.

It took two weeks for an Act to be rushed through Parliament. That fortnight in early May was enough to push the Nore seamen over the brink into mutiny; they thought the Spithead deal was not going to be honoured, so they started unrigging their ships and forming committees in preparation for mutiny. A collection was made among the seamen on ships at the Nore and twenty pounds was raised to send a delegation of four from Sheerness to Portsmouth in order to find out just how reliable the Admiralty promises were.

Finally, on 14 May, the Act, signed by the King, and the guarantee of a pardon were delivered to Portsmouth, and the mutiny at Spithead came to an end in an atmosphere more like a regatta with bands playing and Earl Howe making a triumphal tour round the Fleet displaying the King's signature.

There were two important aspects of the settlement which were to lead to trouble with the Nore mutineers. The first was that the pardon specifically mentioned those who had mutinied up to the date of the settlement – and the Nore men were just beginning their action. The other was that there was no mention on paper of the removal of unpopular officers. The nearest the Admiralty case came to admitting in print that there was a need for improvement on the upper decks was an order to commanders which, while not making specific charges, did include significant paragraphs, such as:

"... Captains and Commanders of the ships and vessels of your squadron never be absent themselves, nor allow any officers under their orders to be absent from on board their respective ships for twenty four hours at a time without our [the Admiralty] permission... That particular attention be paid to the regulations relating to the cutting up of fresh beef, that choice pieces never be purposely selected for the officers... That officers do not select casks of the best wine or spirits for their own use from those intended for the ship's company... Surgeons belonging to ships not to take out of the ship any part of the medicines intended for the use of the sick, but to strictly apply them to the purposes for which they were sent on board..."

The day after the signing of the Spithead agreement, the four delegates from the Nore arrived in Portsmouth rather the worse for wear. They had had to travel to London in order to catch the Portsmouth Coach and, while in London, two of them had been taken by the press gang. It was a measure of their eloquence or, possibly, their ability to bribe, that they managed to talk their way out of the clutches of the press and continue their journey.

Earl Howe gave the Nore seamen copies of the Act of Parliament granting more money and the pardon – which they did not realise did not apply to anyone who mutinied after its date of signature. The four men then took advantage of the celebrations going on and spent a couple of drunken days around the fleshpots of Portsmouth dockyard. Finally a collection had to be made to get them the money to return to Sheerness. One of the four decided that he was tired of the navy, so he deserted and was never seen again.

When the seamen returned to the Nore Fleet Richard Parker, their leader, immediately saw that the pardon was worthless and the other demands not mentioned. The delegates

149

were not popular, but by this time the mutiny at the Nore was a reality and the inconclusive news from Portsmouth strengthened the resolve of the militant leaders who began to extend their demands. Delegates from the ships met on board H.M.S. *Sandwich* and composed a list of conditions that went beyond just wages. Although their demands were formulated six days after the settlement at Spithead, they were obviously unsure if the settlement applied to all, for the first demand was for the increase granted at Portsmouth. They then went on:

"... That every man upon a ship's coming into harbour, shall have liberty (a certain number at a time so as not to injure the ship's duty) to go and see their friends and families, a convenient time to be allowed to each man... That all ships, before they go to sea shall be paid all arrears of wages down to six months, according to the old rules..."

This latter item was an indication that, although the Admiralty claimed that pay was given on time, there was some laxity. Their demands went on:

"... That no officer that has been turned out of His Majesty's ships shall be employed in the same ship again, without the consent of the ship's company... That an indemnification be made any men who run and may now be in His Majesty's naval service, and that they shall not be liable to be taken up as deserters..."

Here the difference between the Spithead demands and those of the Nore were evident. The Sheerness men were making revolutionary demands which would have meant that they had the power to sack any officer and also the right to desert one ship and join another. The final

150

paragraph of their demands read:
"... The committee of delegates of the whole fleet, assembled in council on board His Majesty's ship *Sandwich*, have unanimously agreed that they will not deliver up their charge until the appearance of some of the Lords Commissioners of the Admiralty to ratify the same.
Given on board His Majesty's ship *Sandwich* by the delegates of the fleet, May 20th 1797. Richard Parker, President."

It is possible that if one of the Lords of the Admiralty had gone down to Sheerness at this point to tell the fleet, as Earl Howe had done, face to face, that the raise in pay was all they were getting and offering a pardon, then Parker and the ring leaders would have found themselves standing alone and the mutiny would have been over. But there were those at the Admiralty who thought that the Spithead settlement was too much, attitudes had hardened. The reply from London the next day was "no".

Charles Buckner, Vice Admiral of the White and Commander of the Nore and Medway, sat in his office at Sheerness, afraid to show the unequivocal reply to the mutineers. He could hear the successive hurrahs drifting across the muddy Thames as ships' companies gave three cheers, the rallying cry of the naval rebels. The seamen were assured by the Admiralty that a pardon was offered to them if they returned to duty. They were also assured that the increase in pay was due to them too, but the fever of excitement was running through the fleet; they wanted the sort of victory that the Spithead seamen had won.

One of the first ships to be taken over was H.M.S.*Director*, commanded ironically by

151

Captain Bligh of the notorious *Bounty*; he seemed to be accident prone when it came to mutinies. Bligh was away from the ship attending a court martial on another vessel when his crew took over. As he climbed on deck from the long boat he was greeted by the lower deck delegates, who were demanding the removal of two lieutenants and a sailing master for 'ill usage'. As on many of the mutiny ships there was an uneasy stalemate between officers and crew. The men were respectful to Bligh and were running the ship as usual; he still had control of the arms and the keys to various strong boxes. He sent the 'dismissed' officers below out of the way and there was a truce for a short while, but eventually Bligh found himself on shore at Sheerness writing to the Secretary to the Admiralty and, no doubt, remembering a similar situation in the South Seas:

"... You will please to inform my Lords Commissioners of the Admiralty that this morning about nine o'clock, soon after the return of the delegates from Spithead, they came on board and declared to me they had seen Earl Howe, who had told them all officers were to be removed from their ships who they disapproved of...[this was not true, the mutineers were bluffing]... they were in consequence to inform me in the name of the ship's company that I was to quit the command of the ship and for it to devolve on the First Lieutenant, who they in the same breath ordered to supercede me..

Being without any resource I was obliged to quit the ship. I have stated the whole transaction to Admiral Buckner, and now wait their Lordships' directions, being ready to meet any charge that can be brought against me or such investigations as they think proper to direct. I have reason to believe the whole was originated with the *Sandwich's* crew; hitherto never did a ship's company behave better or did a ship bear more marks of content and correctness.

Mr Purdue, Mr Blaguire, and Mr Eldridge, Midshipman, are also turned on shore for being too much noticed by their Captain and Mr Purdue particularly because he did his duty like a spirited young officer – I know of nothing dishonourable they can be accused of.

Wm.Bligh. "

Unlike the Spithead mutineers, who constantly pleaded loyalty and readiness to set sail if the French broke out of Brest, the Nore strikers were becoming more militant. Parties went ashore and paraded through the streets with red flags and red cockades in their hats. The Chequers Public House in Sheerness became a headquarters for ships' committees to meet. A party seized eight gun boats from Sheerness harbour and sailed them out to the Nore, firing off a few rounds at the walls of Sheerness Fort as they passed. Others took long boats and tried to row up river to Long Reach and Gravesend to persuade the crews of ships anchored there to join the mutiny.

Royalty was also involved in the repercussions of the troubles in the Thames. Princess Charlotte was married to the Prince of Wurtemberg and the frigate *San Fiorenzo* arrived at the Nore to await the Royal couple and carry them off to Germany, but, although the crew of the frigate were not keen to join the mutiny they had no choice. The government realised the danger of implicating Royalty in sailing through a mutinous fleet and suggested that the best route to their new home would be by coach to Harwich and then by a loyal frigate to the

153

continent.

The Delegates of the Whole Fleet at the Nore, as the mutineers called themselves, were by this time clearly under the command of one man, a situation the Spithead men had avoided. Richard Parker was a seaman on board H.M.S. *Sandwich*, where Bligh correctly pinpointed as the birthplace of the dispute. Parker was once a lieutenant in the navy and was courtmartialed for insubordination and demoted to able seaman. He then left the navy and went to live in Scotland, where he married. He later found himself in a debtors' prison and seized the opportunity to rejoin the navy as a 'quota' man for the bounty of £30 which paid his debts. When the need for men was acute, each district or town in the country was given a 'quota', which was the number of men they were to supply for service afloat. These men were supposed to be volunteers and, as such, were given a bounty on joining, but they were frequently either criminals on the run or debtors, like Parker, who needed the money.

Parker was a convincing orator and was better educated than most of his shipmates. He visited ships exhorting their crews to join the mutiny and was not above making these exhortations more graphic by a show of force. The frigates *Clyde* and *San Fiorenzo*, the redundant royal transport, were not joining in with enthusiasm, so Parker sent the *Plyades* to anchor between them. The ships' crews of *Clyde* and *San Fiorenzo* watched the *Plyades* furl its sails and were then surprised to see her gun ports creaking open and her twelve-pounders run out to point ominously, at point blank range, at the two wavering ships. Other opponents of the Delegates, including officers, were sometimes ducked in the sea by being trussed in a hammock and then suspended on a yard rope and allowed to fall into the sea from a yard arm. The victim was then lifted out and ducked again until he was nearly drowned.

There was not complete unity among the Nore mutineers. Quite a few crews were only luke warm about the adventure. The crews of *Sandwich* and *Inflexible* had to exert pressure on the feint hearts to make them continue. The wages had now been raised and the other issues, such as shore leave, prize money and the dismissal of officers, had such little chance of success that it was not worth risking the noose to continue.

It appeared that there might be an end to the dispute when Earl Spencer, one of the Sea Lords, arrived in Sheerness, but he refused to talk directly with the mutineers. His only gesture was to assure the men that the pardon would be granted if they returned to their duties immediately. He also had news of an Act passed by Parliament of the death penalty for those who helped mutineers. The Admiralty sensed that the mutiny was losing its momentum; they moved troops into Sheerness and the Essex coast. All food and other supplies were denied the mutiny ships, officers were ordered ashore. Sheerness became a haven for those ships defying the mutineers and a boom was placed across the Medway entrance.

A few ships began to escape the mutineers. The *Clyde* chopped her cables in the night and quietly drifted away from the guns of *Plyades* when she was out of gunshot range, she put on canvas and sailed into Sheerness. The *San Fiorenzo* secretly took on a pilot and also made a run for it, but missed the tide and was fired upon by other ships while she waited for enough water to enable her to limp into Sheerness.

At this time it was feared that the Dutch would break out of the blockade of the Texel, which was being guarded by ships of the North Sea Fleet based at Yarmouth, but some of Admiral Duncan's North Sea Fleet were also refusing to sail and had come round to the estuary to join the Nore mutiny, where by now the mutineers were in a state of war with the Admiralty. They decided to blockade the Thames, so that no ship could leave to relieve the North Sea squadron. No ship was allowed in or out of the Thames without the permission of Richard Parker. Merchant ships were stopped and forced to anchor; soon there were hundreds riding at anchor off Whitstable, Herne Bay, and Leigh. The wharves of London, normally in a chaos of overcrowding, were beginning to go quiet.

By now it was early June; on 5 June, the official birthday of George III, there was the unusual spectacle of the mutineers and the loyal ships, plus the Sheerness garrison, all dressed in their best uniforms and firing loyal salutes. But on 7 June the mutineers sent a letter to His Majesty containing the threat that the fleet might sail away and join the enemy if their demands were not met. Their letter was a direct appeal to the King, proclaiming their loyalty and their dismay at being branded traitors and outlaws:

"... We have already determined how to act, and should be extremely sorry we should be forced to repose in another Country, which must evidently be the case if we are denounced as Outlaws in our own...

With loyalty we remain,
Your Majesty's dutiful subjects,
Seamen at the Nore."

There was a fear that the mutineers

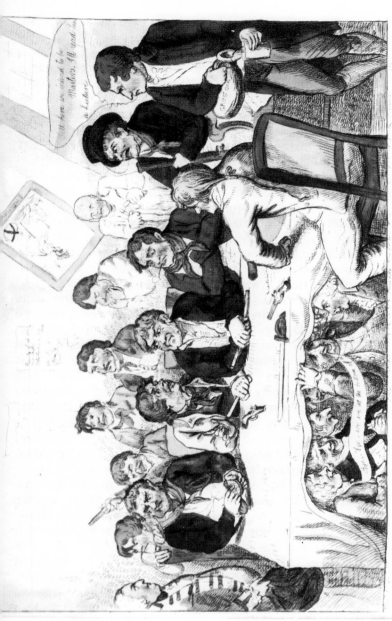

The DELEGATES in COUNCIL or BEGGARS on HORSEBACK

By permission of the National Maritime Museum, Greenwich

would gather their 17 ships and 10,000 men and attack London and plans were made to use colliers as a blockade against them, but by now they were desperate. Food was short, barges were being plundered, farmers reported their sheep stolen from the Kent marshes, and fishermen were liable to have their catch taken.

Delegates began discussing means of escape; some were for sailing to join the enemy, others had the forlorn hope that if they just sailed off to join the British fleets off Brest or the Texel all would be forgotten, a few were for sailing northward round Britain to Ireland and then to a new life in America.

By 10 June no reply had been received from the King and preparations were made to sail, more or less on the basis of every ship for itself. There were many recriminations and fights between those wanting to escape and those who favoured surrender. Men were flogged by the Delegate's committees for 'perjury' against the mutineers' oath. The merchant ships were again allowed to sail for London. Several ships tried to get away from the Fleet and were fired upon by others, some just cut their cables and drifted off to run aground on sandbanks on the Kent and Essex shores. The mutineers reduced their demands to the removal of some officers and a guarantee of a pardon, but it was too late. There was to be no deal.

Ship by ship, the mutiny died; at the signal to up anchor and sail away, not a ship moved. Red flags were lowered and in their place the ensign and the Union Jack returned. On board the *Sandwich*, President of the Delegates of the Fleet at the Nore, Richard Parker, hoisted the white flag of surrender. Delegates were rounded up and taken to prisons and other places of security until there was hardly a locked building in Sheerness without seamen inside its walls awaiting their fate. A proclamation from the Duke of Portland was posted up in Sheerness and other Thames towns:

"Whereas there is reason to believe that Richard Parker, now or late a super-numerary seaman on board H.M.S. *Sandwich*, at the Nore, and who stands charged with diverse acts of mutiny, treason and rebellion, will attempt to make his escape from the said ship, his Majesty for the better discovering and apprehending of the said Richard Parker, is hereby pleased to promise a reward of five hundred pounds, to be paid by the Lords Commissioners of his Majesty's Treasury, to any person or persons who shall apprehend or cause the said Richard Parker to be apprehended, and brought before some of his Majesty's justices of the peace or chief magistrates of the county, town, or place where he shall be apprhended, so that he may be dealt withal, and proceeded against according to the law.

Signed: Portland"

The proclamation was not needed, Parker was brought ashore tied up and under the muzzles of a company of the West Yorks militia. "I expect an impartial trial", he was heard to state.

Parker was clearly going to be scapegoat-in-chief, but others were getting away. The most militant crew throughout the mutiny were those on board H.M.S *Inflexible* running out guns to menace those who looked like surrendering. But in the end there were just twelve men on the *Inflexible* who were for fighting on and they were overcome by their shipmates and put below. They were obviously not locked up, for while the ship was under a white flag and waiting to surrender, the twelve men, under the leadership of John Blake, slipped out of a gun port into three long boats and made a run for it.

The boats hugged the shallow waters where gun boats could not follow them and made their way down river to the open sea. When they got beyond sight of the Nore, they turned into the Swale and, as it was getting dark, arrived in Faversham. Their appearance and obvious gait of seamen would have soon betrayed them to units of the militia who were on the look out for escaping mutineers. They found a small sloop, overcame the men on board her, and ran out of the Swale well camouflaged and heading for Calais, hoping to join the French.

When the escapers reached France they did not receive the welcome they expected; they were put in prison and there was a danger of their being treated as prisoners of war and exchanged, but they were allowed in time to join the crews of French privateers and were able to quietly escape the fate about to catch up with some of their fellow mutineers.

Parker's trial for mutiny opened on 22 June on board H.M.S. *Neptune* anchored near Greenhithe. There were thirteen members of the court ready to hear evidence and pass judgment. Unable to muster so many impartial captains and post captains, the thirteen were made up largely of officers who had been involved in the mutiny in some way – either deposed from their commands or put ashore.

Parker was brought from Maidstone gaol and stood before the long table of thirteen of his officers. His defence was largely concerned with impressing the court that he always treated the officers with respect and his involvement in the mutiny was in order to prevent others from more violent actions:

"...I did all in my power to prevent the bad effects that were likely to arise from this bad temper of the seamen. All my measures were adopted with that view. The proceedings of the fleet would have been much more alarming had I not acted the part I did..."

On the morning of 30 June, Parker was hanged on board H.M.S. *Sandwich* anchored in the mouth of the Medway. All the ships of the fleet had been assembled, together with a large crowd on the banks. Parker's wife, Ann, had come to London from Scotland in the hope of petitioning the Queen for the life of her husband. Mrs Parker hired a boatman to take her out to H.M.S. *Sandwich* on the day of the execution, but she was not allowed on board. She remained in a state of shock in the small boat, bobbing about beside *Sandwich* as her husband was led to the platform built out from the forecastle of the ship, the noose put over his head and his body yanked up on one of the yard ropes which had been so evident during the mutiny.

Trials continued on board H.M.S. *Neptune*; there were about 60 sentences of death, some of which were were commuted to transportation. The number of men who actually followed Parker to their deaths is vague, probably about 35 or 40; others were sentenced to two or three years imprisonment and were sent in chains to the prison hulks moored in the Thames and the Medway. Some of those imprisoned in the hulks were fortunate for the navy still needed men and many a good foretopman was taken from the hulks and sent off to sea again.

Parker's wife, showing a good deal of initiative and determination, organised a body-snatching raid on the graveyard near Sheerness,

161

removed the body of her husband, and transported it to London. She placed the body in an inn called the Hoop and Horseshoe in Queen Street, Tower Hill, while she looked for a burial ground; here it became a curiosity with people coming to view the body. The Home Office got to hear of the removal of Parker's body and snatched it back. They eventually agreed to bury it in the churchyard of St Botolph's at Aldgate, but the crowd got to hear of it and the authorities removed it secretly once more. At last Mrs Parker took her husband's remains to the church of St Mary Matfelon nearby, where it was quietly given the last rituals by the rector.

Attempts were made to prove that the mutinies at the Nore and Spithead were motivated by revolutionary elements, such as Jacobins, London Corresponding Societies, or other political groups, but there was no real proof. Parker or some of the mutineers may have been advised by outsiders, but were probably acting on their own. Their actions simply reflected the mood of late 18th century industrial unrest. As the Thames was the seat of a great deal of that industry, its waters made a logical battleground.

Law & Punishment

How the Law tried to cope by imposing harsh puniishments, trans portation, hanging. The horrors of the prisons. Informers. The prison hulks off the Kent shore.

At certain times in the 18th century there were more than 300 crimes for which a person could be hanged, yet many criminals still managed to thrive because of the chaotic state of law enforcement. As described earlier, there was no organised police force and little enthusiasm for creating one. Many law officials were in positions for which they had paid a substantial sum of money; they had bought their jobs and were concerned primarily in making their investment show a good profit.

The few reformers who were uneasy about the practice of purchasing law positions had their protests brushed aside because many towns, including London, could not afford to pay for a well organised law enforcement service nor an honest judiciary. The trading justices and the corrupt or unwilling constables were no deterrent to crime. Rather than improve the administration of law and justice, Government simply passed more severe laws and made hanging and transportation the sentence for more offences. Most of the new capital offences were for theft or damage to property – to appease the merchants and property owners who complained about the losses from their warehouses and homes and damage to their houses by rioters.

The effect of the harsher sentences was not as expected; juries and justices tended not to convict a person for a petty theft if they could help it, for it often meant that the accused would be executed for stealing a handkerchief or a cabbage, so the number of executions did not increase in proportion to the capital offences.

Before a person could be brought to trial he had to be caught. Although the public were supposed to join in the hue and cry to help catch thieves, in the riverside communities there were so many thieves that it was difficult to raise what was known as a 'posse comitatum' to uphold the law. The areas of riverside London, such as The Mint on the south bank or Alsatia, which housed mainly criminals, also had 'shelterers' whose job it was to protect criminals. Bailiffs were especially vulnerable to attack from shelterers, who would hold their own courts and administer punishments on bailiffs bold enough to venture into the area. These punishments usually took the form of a ducking at the local pump or open sewer. The few determined attempts to arrest criminals or debtors usually resulted in pitched battles.

In 1705 an attempt by constables to arrest a debtor was met by an attack from the shelterers and other residents of the Mint. The man was eventually taken after 20 constables and four justices of the peace fought a battle in the streets.

To have someone charged with a crime usually meant that the aggrieved party had to take out a private prosecution. The justice machine was passive until it had a criminal presented for judgement. There was little investigation of crime, therefore the criminals actually caught and charged were predominantly those discovered by customs or watchmen on the quays. They were usually those who did not have the wit or the friends to aid their escape.

In October, 1799, George Haynes was indicted for stealing a pound of wool, value one shilling. Constable John Seally saw Haynes on Galley Quay pick up the wool as it fell from a hole in a 200 lb bale. The Common Serjeant sentenced Haynes to be whipped at the place of his crime. Thomas Jones was another petty thief who was caught stuffing sugar into his shirt and trousers on Smart's Quay; for the seven pounds of sugar he stole he received a sentence of seven years' transportation. These two men were caught red-handed, but if there had been some doubt and they had put up a spirited defence, declaring their innocence, they may have been able to sway the judges or the jury for, although sentences were harsh, many judges were sympathetic to a tale of woe or misfortune. They frequently took a benign attitude and, rather than commit someone to transportation or harsh punishment, they took a more patronising view and showed mercy.

Constables, too, sometimes behaved in a conciliatory fashion, especially in the country districts down river. Their role was often as peacemakers or even advocates on behalf of the criminal. William Bart and Robert Raisly were moving 600 lbs of smuggled tobacco from the river north into Essex one morning when they stopped at an inn at Springfield. Unfortunately for them, James Gladwin, the local butcher, was drinking at the inn and he suspected that the bundles in the smugglers' cart contained bodies. When Mr Gladwin and some other locals challenged the two smugglers, they first refused to open the bundles, but a local excise officer called at the inn and slit open the bundles with his knife to reveal tobacco. Then John Dawson, the Parish Constable, was called and it seems that he and two of the locals took Mr Gladwin and the Excise man away from the others and tried to persuade them to let the men hitch up their horses and drive on, but butcher Gladwin was an upright citizen and would not tolerate such behaviour. So, in spite of the Constable's attempts to smooth things over and mediate, Bart and Raisly were each gaoled until they could pay H.M.Customs £100 as a bond against their future behaviour.

Although the upright Mr Gladwin would look upon himself as a person doing his duty, there is a note from the Controller of Customs in the Essex Records Office to the effect that he was entitled to a reward, if he cared to apply for it. He was looked upon as one of the vast army of informers who brought most criminals to book. The law passively waited for aggrieved citizens to swear out warrants or for informers to denounce criminals.

As well as the genuine law-abiding citizen who told of a crime he had discovered, there were those who made a precarious living from informing. Like the trading justices, they took advantage of the inadequacies of the law. Henry Fielding in his *Extracts from the Penal Law* describes informers thus:

"... In most of our penal laws part of the penalty is given to the informer: this has made the character of an informer not only odious but dangerous, and seldom or ever pro-duces any but the most disreputable witnesses..."

This is an opinion still prevailing today, nevertheless informers were regularly used, as we saw from the activities of Mr Penprice in Chapter 3. There seemed to be less inhibition about offering bribes for information. In 1765 the West India Company published an advertisement setting out their terms for those who 'discovered' any pilfering from their ships:

"... every person making such discovery, shall be intitled to a reward of forty shillings, on the conviction of every such offender. And that every person who shall discover as aforesaid, any buyer or receiver of such stolen goods, knowing them to be stolen, shall be intitled to a reward of twenty pounds on conviction of every such buyer or receiver..."

In the correspondence of Mr Collier, the Surveyor General of Riding Officers in Kent, there are letters indicating the value of informers to the undermanned Customs Service. He refers to the Reverend Patten of Whitstable, who informed him when smuggling crews passed through the town. Collier's papers also illustrate how, once an informer gives his information, he then has to be protected, humoured and threatened in order to be available for a later court appearance.

An informer named Thomas Pettet, who informed against a William Weston and others was told by Collier to be available to attend the Assizes a few months thence. In Collier's file there are worried letters from Pettet. Firstly, he is concerned that his business as a tailor is foundering and, secondly, he is afraid, understandably, that Weston's friends will attack him. In letters showing the strange colloquial spelling of the literate artisan he expresses his fears and frequently asks for money. In a letter to Collier dated 6 December, 1736, he acknowledges receipt of 30 shillings and continues in a strange mixture of bravado and apprehension, asking if any more smugglers have been caught, presumably he felt safer if as many as possible are behind bars:

"... If I should be smelt out i moust louck to my selfe..."

but later he expresses his determination to appear against the smugglers, vowing that he will:

"... stick clouse to them and all as thear shourt to thear back..."

Three weeks later there is another letter asking for more money, but sounding determined to appear at the Assizes "for", he says:

"... they be fetheard bourds, and it will be wourth wile to plouck them, but to go before one of our justeses i was good nouck [knock] my hed against the wall for cissing [kissing] goues by favear..."

A few weeks later he is again writing to ask for more money to buy new clothes in order to attend the Assizes, pleading that the evidence would be more plausible if presented by someone who would "appear clean and genteel..."

He goes on to protest that he fears no man, pays all his dues, goes to church regularly, keeps good company, and is well respected in his village. A week later another letter is less confident, he is complaining that one of Mr Collier's servants has revealed his treachery to the smugglers who have threatened:

"... to make a hole for the sun to shine through him..."

He also complains that one of the men he informed against has evidence that he was elsewhere. This makes poor Pettet fear that he will be charged with perjury should the jury believe the smuggler.

The very real danger that informers risked, especially from locals who were sympathetic to the smugglers, was attack from mobs of supporters. In January, 1751, Excise Officer John Lidgate was talking in the street in Chatham to one of his informers, John Brewer. Suddenly they found themselves surrounded by a mob of people who began to attack them with sticks. Lidgate and Brewer took to their heels and the mob followed, throwing stones and crying out:

"... Informers, they ought to be hanged, it is no sin to kill them..."

At a time of riot householders closed and barred their doors and windows, but Lidgate and Brewer sought refuge in the house of Mr and Mrs Alexander Garner. Mr Garner removed the bar from the door to let the fugitives in, but the mob were so close behind that he had to beat off the vanguard with the iron bar as they tried to force their way into the house. While the fight at the door was going on, some of the crowd were throwing stones, one of which struck Mrs Garner, knocking her unconscious. Meanwhile, Officer Lidgate and his informer escaped out of the back of the house and were able to take refuge in another house until the mob dispersed.

The evidence from some 18th century informers gives an insight into some of the activities of the more sophisticated criminals involved in cheating the government out of customs duties.

Part of wine merchant Robert Redhead's business was to buy large quantities of prize spirits. These prize spirits were smuggled wines and spirits which had been seized by the customs, who then re-sold them to merchants who undertook to export them and thereby did not have to pay any duty. Mr Redhead found he could make far more money by selling the liquor at home. Provided he exported the same number of casks or hogsheads as he purchased from the prize spirit sale the customs were not alerted to any misdemeanour. So Mr Redhead instructed his clerks and cellarmen to substitute water for the gin and water flavoured with cayenne pepper for the brandy.

Eventually George Lay, one of Mr Redhead's clerks, was persuaded to turn informer. How this came about is not clear from the evidence. There were probably a series of fierce complaints from the recipients of the cayenne water masquerading as brandy which seems to have been exported to the Baltic ports. Mr Redhead probably thought the deception would be blamed upon some unknown thief in transit. This was a naive belief because the tale-telling clerk, George Lay, described the extent of the theft in his evidence:

"... got up early the next morning for the purpose of getting into the said last mentioned vault or warehouse and that they the said Robert Redhead, Joseph Saunders, William Hyder, and he this deponent accordingly got up between four and five o'clock the next morning and went down and forced down some of the boards of a partition at the bottom of a staircase by which the communication between the said vault or warehouse and the said Robert Redhead's house had before been blocked up... and by that means they entered the said prize vault or warehouse and then and at different times afterwards drew off clandestinely from the said casks or puncheons nearly the whole of the fifty puncheons of prize geneva and also eighty seven puncheons of prize brandy..."
A puncheon held between 70 and 120 gallons, so their thieving was big business.

Some informers were especially recruited

from debtors' prisons and paid according to the information they provided. These people were known as 'Missionaries' and were mostly the dregs of the misfits and idiots of the waterside, or were so desperate to get out of gaol they were willing to become informers. They were sent out into the underworld and told to listen and report what was going on. Many of these missionaries found themselves in a worse state than when they were in prison. Few of them were smart enough to carry on their spying undetected for very long. Many were sooner or later found floating in the Thames. Their information was not reliable, as they often found it safer and easier to invent information which they thought would please their pay-masters.

A more reliable informant was the well-meaning amateur, like Nancy of Deptford. She wrote to the Captain of a man of war anchored in the Thames:

"... Captain Barrington sir, their is a deserter of yours at the upper water gate. Lives at the sine of the Mantion House. He is an Irishman, gose by the name of Youe [Hugh] Mackmullins and is trying to ruing a wido and three children for he has insenuated into the old woman's faver so far that she must sartingly come to poverty, and you by sarching the cooks will find what I have related to be true and much oblige the hole parish of St Pickles Deptford..."

Not all informers were unsuccessful wretches from prison; the most notoriously successful was Jonathan Wild, known as a 'thief taker'. He ran a private force of informers and undertook to bring criminals to justice; unfort-unately he was probably the biggest criminal of them all. He organised gangs of thieves, he was a receiver of stolen goods, he was a brothel keeper. He had such a thriving empire of thieves that he bought a sloop to transport the stolen goods to the continent. His reputation as a thief taker was built up by his practice of denouncing rivals and employees who had crossed him. His misdeeds caught up with him in 1725, when he was finally caught by his own methods and hanged for receiving stolen property.

It was said that when Jonathan Wild was taken to be hanged there was an unusually enthusiastic crowd at Tyburn to see him 'turned off'. This was probably because he had made so many enemies among the underworld fraternity, for his most lucrative activity was the 'discovery' of stolen property and its return to the rightful owner in an elaborate routine of passing the property through panels in the wall in return for a sum of money, a form of ransom which he shared with the thief. The thief received the smaller share and, if he objected, he was turned over to justice. So the crowd to watch Wild hanged was probably made up of many of his victims, criminal and otherwise.

There were public hangings at Tyburn and at Execution Dock, Wapping, which went on until the 1780s. Although many death sentences were commuted, there was still a steady number for the hangman to deal with. Those living on the route between Newgate and Tyburn were familiar with the parade of wretched prisoners making their last journey; the better off in a coach, others on the back of a horse-drawn cart.

To some of the condemned even this journey would have been a relief after the horrors of Newgate Prison, sited where the present Old Bailey Court stands. It was a gaunt, black building on two sides of Newgate Street

172

with a 60 foot tower spanning across the top of the City Gate. The cells were built for security and such refinements as adequate light and air were not considered. The secure cells were in galleries whose heavy timber was home for anything that could crawl and feed off the inmates, for there was precious little waste food. The privileged ones who were accomodated in the Press Yard could glimpse the sun at midday on fine summer days, but they paid very highly for that privilege. As much as £500 down payment and £1 per week for furniture was the going rate, plus extras for 'garnish', such as edible food or extra chairs. Those without money or friends spent their sentence in 'The Hold', a large underground dungeon where the cockroaches crackled beneath the feet like autumn leaves as you stumbled about in the near darkness.

James Hardy Vaux, in his memoirs, tells of his first day in Newgate:

"... I was roused by the turnkey, at a late hour in the morning. This personage now behaved with some civility and let me know that if I had any money I might be supplied with a good breakfast, at the same time tossing on the bed a small loaf (about 14 ozs) of bread which he told me was the daily allowance of the prison. I gladly accepted his offer, and desired to have some tea... I continued to have three tolerable meals every day during my stay, but I paid for each on delivery, and through the nose..."

A hundred or so prisons of various sorts were dotted about London in the 18th century. Blackfriars had The Fleet, The Ludgate and The Bridewell House of Correction, as well as Newgate a few hundred yards up the hill. Their grim presence, combined with the stench from

173

the filth of the Fleet River flowing down to the Thames and the unsavoury population of the area, made it a place for the timid to avoid. The relatives of the inmates of the prisons tended to gather in the gin shops and inns of the district or seek accomodation in the slums nearby.

The prisons themselves were not the regimented lock-ups of today. For those who could pay the bribes, visitors were allowed in at all times. Drink was available to all who could pay; each prison had a beer tap which the Keeper of the prison operated as one of his many perks. In 1751, an Act was passed forbidding the sale of spirits in prisons, but it was largely ignored. It was not uncommon for the well-off prisoners to throw a party, or even a dance, complete with invitations:

"... You are invited to Mr ... Public Free and Easy Society at Newgate Prison..." The noise of drunkenness, fighting and debauchery rang through the prisons every night, but for the most part they were places of despair, with harsh punishments for those who did not conform or have money. There was also the before-dawn rattle of chains and cursing as those who were to be transported were led out to Blackfriars to be put on board barges for the down river journey from which many never returned.

Transportation of felons was a convenient way of both ridding the country of criminals and providing cheap labour for the colonies in the Caribbean and America. It began with an Act in the reign of Queen Elizabeth in 1597 "for the punishment of rogues, vagabonds, and sturdy beggars". How many were shipped abroad and how many of those were real criminals it is impossible to say. Although many found themselves in slavery, others, especially those with

174

money who were able to buy themselves comforts on the journey, found that life in Virginia or Maryland was better than in England. Some prospered, as did Defoe's fictional characters, Moll Flanders and Colonel Jack.

As mentioned earlier, many volunteered to emigrate. They may have been duped by unscrupulous agents or ship's captains, but many of them formed the roots of successful American planter families. So successful were some of these immigrants, voluntary or otherwise, that by the 1760s and 70s there was a substantial anti-British feeling among the settlers, many of whom were enemies of the Georges, such as Jacobites and victims of purges after the '45 Rebellion. Their cause was advanced by successive attempts to impose more taxation and trade restrictions. This finally resulted in the War of Independence and the eventual defeat of the British, but long before this, in 1770, only Maryland would accept transported convicts and Britain was faced with the dilemma of what to do with those sentenced to be transported. A 'temporary' solution was found until the rebels across the Atlantic could be dealt with. Those sentenced to transportation, many of whom had been reprieved from hanging, were to be imprisoned in disused ships anchored in the Thames and on the south coast, where they could be used as labour on shore works. Those sentenced to transportation from London were carried no further than Woolwich, where they spent their sentences chained like animals in the prison hulks anchored off the mud flats of the south Thames shore.

The hard labour they had to perform was the digging and dredging of the foreshore for the construction of the Woolwich Arsenal at a

175

place called The Warren.

It was a popular sightseeing trip for the boatmen to take people to see the convicts at work on The Warren, or to sail near the hulks and peer into the barred ports. Eventually a wall was built on the land side of The Warren to discourage sightseers. 'A gentleman' describes the scene in *The Scots Magazine*:

"... those objects who have fetters on each leg, with a chain between, that ties variously, some round their middle, other upright to the throat. Some are chained two and two; and others, whose crimes have been enormous, with heavy fetters. Six or seven are continually walking about with them with drawn cutlasses, to prevent their escape and likewise to prevent idleness..."

The more privileged could be taken on board to look down on the convicts from the safety of the quarter deck. It was highly unlikely that visitors ever saw below decks, where even the officers were reluctant to go. James Hardy Vaux, who graduated from Newgate to the hulks describes the scene:

"... of all the shocking scenes I had ever beheld, this was the most distressing. There were confined in this floating dungeon nearly 600 men, most of them double ironed; and the reader may conceive the horrible effects arising from the continual rattling of chains, the filth and vermin naturally produced by such a crowd of miserable inhabitants, the oaths and execrations constantly heard among them; and above all from the shocking necessity of associating and communicating more or less with so depraved a set of beings..."

New prisoners were confined to the lowest deck which was always damp and airless. As the prisoner proved he was well behaved, he

176

Prison hulk at Deptford, 1826

was rewarded by promotion to decks higher in the ship, the upper deck being the most sought after. On arrival the prisoners were stripped of their clothes, doused in cold water and then fitted out with a suit of loose fitting 'slops' similar to those worn by Royal Navy sailors. They were then fitted with chains, the more dangerous the criminal was regarded, the more chains he had to carry.

The conditions below decks were very overcrowded; as many as 500 men packed into one deck. At first the men slept on platforms, but as more convicts arrived they had to sleep in hammocks; in two tiers, one above the other, each with a space 6 feet by 20 inches. At the peak of overcrowding many had not even a hammock; they slept where they could on the floor.

In winter prisoners were shut below decks for 8 or 9 hours. Officers and guards were afraid to go down among them unless it was urgently necessary. One or two prisoners on each deck were designated boatswain's mates and had to call out "all's well" at certain times in the night. The atmosphere below decks was horrific, even in winter with unglazed ports it became unbearably hot. When the hatches were opened in the mornings no one could descend into the lower decks until the air had cleared.

The bad conditions were brought about partly by the system of sub-contracting the running of the hulks to private individuals. Because it was anticipated that the hulks would only be a temporary measure, the Act of Parliament setting them up only ran for a year. but had subsequently to be renewed annually until 1856. Once the hulks were in being, they were found to be a useful source of cheap labour for the hard work of dredging the shore and driving piles in the wet and often cold weather. From their setting up in 1776. there seems to have been very little interest in them from the Government or the public at large.

The Thames hulks were at first under the supervision of the Middlesex Justices. Their concern was to avoid too much expense, so they employed an overseer, Duncan Campbell. assisted by his brother Neil, who seem to be bigger criminals than most of those on the hulks. The Campbells took over the entire setting up and running of the Thames prison hulks; they had previously been engaged in the transportation to the colonies, so they knew something of the business of providing the minimum of food and accomodation to sustain life. They charged £32 per year for each convict and supplied their own ships at the beginning. The hulks soon became known ironically as 'Campbell's Academy'. The Campbells took on every task concerning the hulks, at a fee. They even looked after the dead by buying a piece of ground in Woolwich where their officers supervised the burial of the men who died, many of whom mysteriously found their way into the hands of the medical profession after burial.

The food supplied was the minimum in quality and quantity to allow the men the strength to work; weak soup made from bullocks' heads and other condemned cattle sent down from London. There was also 'burgoo', a gruel of oatmeal and barley. To drink they had about two quarts of beer a week – or the Thames water.

Because the hulks began life as a temporary measure, they seem to have escaped most of the attention of the reformers who were trying to improve prison conditions. When the Act came up for renewal in 1777, Howard, the prison reformer, and his supporters managed to get an enquiry started under the Chairmanship of Sir Charles Bunbury. This and subsequent committees took their evidence from witnesses supplied by the Campbells and concluded that "the hulks are convenient, airy, and healthy."

The Chaplains who were appointed did not take their duties very seriously; during the frequent outbreaks of typhus they officiated at funerals from the safety of the ships, waving a handkerchief to the burial party on shore when they had finished their 'graveside' prayers.

The general public's attitude was that if the convicts were working 8 or 9 hours a day, this was less than most of the working class population and the cost of keeping them in the hulks was more than a free labourer earned, so the unfortunate convicts had few friends to plead their case.

Some escaped, especially in the early years, but this was not easy. The ships were anchored near the Kent shore where it was easier to summon up militia to give chase. Those who could saw through their chains and make for the Essex side of the river stood a greater chance of avoiding capture as the Essex shore at that point was less populous.

In 1776, soon after the hulks were set up, five of the prisoners seized the arms chest of the *Justitia* one of the ships used. They drove the guards below and escaped in a boat, but the guards fired on them, killing two and wounding another. Later that year, twenty-two surprised the Captain and managed to escape to the north bank. They were attacked at East Ham by a party of sailors, but a few managed to reach Epping Forest and were not seen again.

The hulks may have been a temporary

measure when they were first set up, but the loss of the American colonies and the attraction of a ready supply of labour soon made the presence of those black, mastless prisons a more permanent fixture on the Thames. In 1787 convicts were being sent out to Australia, but still the hulks remained. In fact, more were installed in the Medway in the 19th century to accomodate French prisoners of war. As if the Thames did not provide a living for enough criminals, it was also housing those from elsewhere.

In time new prisons on land were built and the number of men sent to the hulks gradually reduced, until in 1856, the last of the prisoners were transferred to Chatham from the remaining three hulks moored at Woolwich. It is probable that the ships were in such a poor condition that they were just left to rot away. The last mention of them was when one of them caught fire and was completely burned out in June 1857

The New Century

Enclosed docks. The new River Police. The Coast Guard service. Coffee houses competed with pubs and innkeepers restricted from acting as labour agents

The criminals who operated on the Thames in the late 18th century were not to know that the situation of near anarchy was coming to an end. The river was to continue to provide pickings for the dishonest, and still does today, but the inadequate and disorganised attempts to combat crime were slowly being supplanted by more professional and determined measures.

Ship owners were losing hundred of thousands of pounds annually. The Government's high tariffs spawned more and more smugglers and the increasing Thameside population was becoming heavily infiltrated by criminals who terrorised and degraded communities. They were beginning to drive out the more law-abiding citizens who settled away from the river and left the quays and wharves to become criminal ghettos.

In the final decade of the century there was little sign of significant action to overcome the river crime, but there was a general awareness of the need to improve social conditions. Hangings were conducted at Newgate and there was no longer the degrading spectacle of the condemned being paraded through the streets to

Tyburn to 'go west' or to 'dangle on the Sheriff's tree', as the cant terms called it.

Street lighting was improving by the exhortations and bullyings of householders to put lanterns outside their houses. Building regulations were being more vigorously enforced. But there was still a long way to go before conditions for the poor showed any sign of improvement, crime still offered the surest means of relieving their poverty.

There were many pamphlets and appeals for legislation to try to curb the hold the publican had over the riverside poor. Attempts were made to bar publicans from being constables and to abolish the practice of pay tables in pubs. This was not successful until well into the next century. Reformers tried to call attention to the evils of the ale house and the gin shop; their efforts made people welcome the new coffee shops when they began to appear. The tax on coffee was reduced in 1808 and coffee shops became attractive for artisans, especially if they could read, for one of the attractions of the coffee shop and coffee house was the provision of newspapers and reviews which were relatively expensive for individuals to buy.

However, publicans continued to act as coal undertakers and many of them exploited the coal heavers for years. They also operated dubious box clubs and friendly societies.

As the 19th century began, smuggling was booming. Britain was at war with France and Holland, high taxes were needed, so too were ships and seamen; there was little time or money to improve the Customs Service. But the smuggler was enjoying the last years of relative freedom, slowly but surely the Government was getting round to devising more effective pre-

183

ventive measures. In 1818 the Coastal Blockade
was initiated with a chain of look-out posts
within hailing distance of each other. It was
intended to use seamen, but few came forward,
so the personnel was made up of landsmen,
mainly Irish. They soon began colluding with the
smugglers or deserting under threats. The idea
was an advance, in that it accepted the need
for more officers, but it did not take into
account the local strength of the smugglers. The
first significant move to combat smuggling was
when the Government began to reduce some of
the tariffs. Eventually the number of commodities bearing duty was reduced from 1,400 to
30.

In 1829 another attempt at a coastal
watch was tried; the Coast Guard was formed
with an efficient cutter service. A couple of
years later the Coast Guard was taken over by
the Admiralty and was used, not only to combat
smuggling, but as a naval reserve under the
command of serving naval officers. By the 1830s
armed gangs were rarely encountered. The
reduction of the customs tariff and a more
efficient coast watch made smuggling less
attractive. There were also many Royal Naval
seamen and officers available after the defeat
of Napoleon; the fleet did not need them. so
they frequently joined the Coast Guard.

The new force of professionals showed up
the weaknesses of the creaking, hidebound
Customs Service with its insecure and largely
unsupported officers on the coast vainly trying
to keep up with the increase in skill and
sophistication of the smuggler. The Customs
House executives were still behaving like 17th
century gentry. Those who did not buy their
positions often had them as a gift by a grateful
Government for other services. Many had no

duties whatsoever, others left the work to their clerks. When they wanted a holiday, the senior officers could command the use of a 10-oared long boat complete with liveried oarsmen.

There was also the practice of buying one's post and then turning it into a profit as soon as possible by exacting fees and gratuities. Listed against the remunerations of the Receiver General of Customs is the sum of £100 per year as 'compliments on salaries and debentures', which meant that other officers and merchants left him tips. Landing waiters were expected to make £220 per year in fees and gratuities - three times their salaries - these fees they then had to pay to their superiors in an elaborate graded scale.

In its working hours the Customs Service was hardly energetic. Clerks worked from 9 a.m. until 12 noon. Searchers from 9 a.m. till 4 with a two and a half hour lunch break; and there were 45 holy days and feast days in the year when they did not work.

If there was a watershed in the fight against Thames criminals, it was the formation of the West India Merchants' Marine Police Institute. In 1798 a committee of West India merchants decided that their huge losses of thousands of pounds a year by pilfering was too much to bear. They asked Magistrate Patrick Colquhoun, who had been campaigning for a river police force, to form the Marine Police Institute.

On 2 July, 1798, the first police office was opened at No. 259, Wapping New Stairs, financed jointly by the West India merchants' ships masters and the Government.

It was Colquhoun's idea to make the force honest and effective from the beginning. There were 62 officers consisting of constables,

185

surveyors and guards, who would supervise the eight hundred or so lumpers working the ships. He saw the task as difficult:

"... The task was arduous – but as resolution and attention were to be opposed to long habits of turpitude, the difficulties were to be overcome by establishing an accurate system, and by following it up with vigour and perseverance..."

Colquhoun was aware that he needed to instill some sense of responsibility into his men:

"... with the strongest injunctions to conduct themselves with purity, attention, prudence and discretion – warning them of the vigilance with which their conduct would be watched, and the infamy and disgrace which would unquestionably follow any depature from the line of rectitude they had solemnly sworn to pursue, in case of detection, which from the system of checks which was established, was rendered unavoidable..."

Colquhoun also insisted that the service should be under the direction of a magistrate who would be always available to prefer instant charges. By this means his police service would not fall foul of the corruption attached to the infamous trading justices. The magistrate he chose to be in charge of the Marine Police Institute was Harriot, the Essex man who had begged a voyage home from France with smuggler Blyth.

The effect of the new Marine Police Institute, even though it was confined to West India ships, was immediate. In the first year Colquhoun claimed that the losses from the ships was reduced to one fiftieth of the previous year. Lumpers who came on board the ships to unload were confronted with a declaration entitled *Caution Against Pillage. and Plunder*'.

186

which was nailed to the mast. The Marine Police Officer was instructed to read out the regulations regarding unloading. On more than o, e occasion the lumpers left the ship immediately they realised that their opportunities for plunder would be curtailed. It was also noticed that lightermen, who usually remained with their barges beside the ships, left them when they knew there were Marine Police on board. The coopers even demanded more money in lieu of the 'perks' which they were losing.

It was soon realised on the waterfront that the Marine Police were far more efficient than the Customs Service or the futile watchmen. One of their first 'catches' was Samuel Wright, a Limehouse coal dealer, who found himself in the dock at the Old Bailey together with three others, a customs clerk and two excise men.

At 11 o'clock on the night of 30 August, barely two months after the Marine Police was formed, two boats under the command of Surveyor John Gottey were quietly paddling along the north bank of the Thames, in the dark shadows of the waterside buildings near Radcliff Cross, Limehouse. They saw a boat with two oarsmen and a passenger. The police boats left the shadows and challenged the other boat which immediately began to pull away from them toward the south side. Gottey goes on:

"... by the waving of the water under her bow which I could see by the light of the moon, I conceived that something was thrown overboard, I rowed immediately to the place and took in a bag of coffee from out of the water..."

Eventually Mr Wright's boat was caught with a boat hook and forced to stop. He refused to go to the police office in Gottey's boat:

"... I then took hold of him by the collar, and, by the assistance of my men, I took him by force into my boat and we took him to the Marine Police office, just by Wapping New Stairs..."

Wright's defence when he was brought to trial was that he was under the impression that the coffee, five bags in all, was 'private adventure' that was legitimately carried by the crew for their own trading.

The Mate of a ship called *The Three Sisters* from where Wright's boat was heading, gave evidence that the customs men had offered him money to allow them to organise the opening of some coffee bags in the cargo. "Feeling the pressure on me from the wants of my family", the Mate appeared to agree to let them break into the cargo. He gave evidence against the accused, presumably this was why he was not charged. When cross examined, he admitted he had once been the skipper of a slaving ship, but had left because of a discrepancy in the accounts. Not an ideal witness, but good enough to get two of the customs men sentenced to death. Mr Wright was acquitted, his defence of handling 'private adventure' being accepted. If he was innocent, it seems odd that he was doing business at 11 o'clock at night and that he tried to escape throwing the coffee beans overboard.

This case was probably the West India Marine Police's first successful prosecution and was the forerunner of many more. Other ship owners and merchants were soon seeking that the Marine Police be extended to their wharves. This was soon done and was the beginning of the Thames River Police as we know it today. The Admiralty saw the improvement and the Commissioners of the Navy wrote to Colquhoun:

"... The Commissioners of the Navy, having an intention of applying to Parliament, to extend and amend the laws for preventing the embezzlement and stealing of His Majesty's naval stores, and having directed me in preparing the intended Bill... if you will at your leisure furnish me with any hints upon the subject which may have occurred to you... and which you think may be worthy the attention of the Legislature..."

Although Colquhoun's river police force was soon accepted by the merchants and ship masters, it built up a good deal of animosity among the lumpers and coal heavers, who represented a widely held view among the population that professional police forces were a danger to liberty. It is likely that the coal heavers and lumpers had a special reason to dislike the Marine Police in view of the effect they had on illicit incomes. An incident in Wapping one night in October, 1799, shows how Colquhoun's police force did not have too smooth a beginning.

Two coal heavers and a waterman's boy were arrested and taken to the Marine Police office to appear before the magistrate for stealing coal. They were convicted and fined forty shillings each. As they left the police office, a mob gathered outside protesting and throwing stones. They were quite determined, for the stones they were throwing were from the road and were those large cobble stones weighing about twenty pounds each. They broke all the windows of the Marine Police office and the magistrates and officers inside could hear them calling out that they were going to kill those inside.

One of the police officers fired a pistol out of the window which, it was later found out, killed one of the rioters; the rest fled a few yards down the road to hide in Dung Wharf, an alley leading down to the Thames. The magistrates went out to read the Riot Act, but were driven in again by a further attack of stones. During this fracas it was claimed that a shot was fired by the rioters killing one of the police helpers named Gabriel Franks. A man, who seems to have been chosen at random from the mob, was charged with the murder. The indictment reads:

"... not that any evidence can be offered to you that he discharged the pistol by which Franks was killed, but that he was an active man in the riot, encouraging and inciting it..."

James Eyres was eventually convicted for the murder and sentenced to death. His defence was that the rioters had no weapons and that the shot came from those inside the police office, but he seems to have taken his sentence philosophically, for, when the Judge said:

"... Prisoner, may the Lord have mercy on your soul..."

he answered:

"...Amen, I hope he will..."

There was no sudden dramatic change as the 18th century ended and the 19th began, but we can see that the 18th century saw the peak of lawlessness on the river and, as it came to a close, things were starting to improve. The criminals' freedom of movement was being blocked in more and more ways. The working population of the riverside did not see thieving as the easiest way to earn more money. Increasing efforts directed towards industrialisation took the place of war effort after the defeat of Napoleon. The building of the enclosed docks was commenced in places north and south of the Thames. More professional policing, on the shore as well as the river, soon overcame the fears of the public about their liberty being curtailed. Crime and poor social conditions remained in some form, but never more on the same scale as during the 1700s.

BIBLIOGRAPHY

Old Bailey Sessions Papers
Various accounts by the Ordinaries of Newgate
The Annual Register
The Gentleman's Magazine
The Burney collection of 18th century newspapers
The newspaper collection in the Beaney Institute Library, Canterbury.
Parliamentary Papers and Commons Journals

Collection of Statutes Now in Force Related to the Customs collected by Sir Willam Musgrave, 1780

The Public Records Office: Assizes accounts; Plea rolls; King's Bench Records; Admiralty and Treasury Papers

Victoria History of Kent

Victoria History of Essex

David Phillipson: Smuggling - a history...

F Nichols: Honest thieves

E Keble Chatterton: King's Cutters & smugglers

Elizabeth Hoon: The Organisation of the English Customs system, 1696-1786

Ralph Davis: The Rise of the English shipping industry in the 17th & 18th centuries

Jack Lindsay: The Monster City

A F T Brown, editor: Essex people, 1750-1900

P Benton: History of the Rochford Hundred

K C Newton: Essex and the sea

Southend Public Library: Old Leigh

M D George: London life in the 18th century

J W Bready: England before and after Wesley

Harvey Benham: Once upon a tide

J Carswell: From Revolution to Revolution

R Douglas Brown: The Port of London

John Pudney: London's docks

Patrick Colquhoun: A Treatise on the Commerce and Police of the River Thames

W C Finch: Medway River and Valley

George Bishop: Observations, Remarks, and Means to prevent smuggling

Lord Teignmouth & Charles G Harpur: The smugglers

Eric Patridge & F Grose: A Classical Dictionary of the vulgar tongue

Henry Alton & Henry Holland: King's Customs

Neville Williams: Contraband cargoes

Henry Crouch: A Complete guide to Officers of H.M.Customs

History of the Isle of Sheppey
R Finn: The Kent Coast blockade
A & E Wroth: London Pleasure gardens
R Rigden: The floating prisons of Woolwich...
William Branch Johnson: The English prison hulks
Nicholas Barton: The lost rivers of London
Hugh Phillips: The Thames about 1750
Henry Mayhew: London labour and London poor
H Humpherus: History of the Watermen's Co.
R Mitchell & M Leys: History of London life
Henry Fielding: A treatise on the Office of
        Constable
Henry Fielding: Covent Garden Journal
Christopher Hibbert: London
J S Cockburn, editor:Crime in England 1550-1800
John Newton: Journal of a slave trader
Gerard Howson: Thief Taker General
J R Hutchinson: The Press Gang afloat & ashore
Donald Rumbelow: History of police and crime
        in the City of London
Douglas Hay, et al: Albion's fatal tree
James Dugan: The Great Mutiny
W J Neal: History of the Nore Mutiny
Daniel Defoe: A Tour through the Whole Island
        of Great Britain
Samuel Richardson: Familiar letters on
        important occasions
Max Beloff: Public Order & popular disturbances
N Ward: London spy
Sir Leon Radzinowicz: History of the English
        Criminal Law & its administration
Bracebridge Hemyng: Secret of the River
William Addison: The Thames Estuary
The Collier Papers in the Kent County Records
        Office, Maidstone
Trial affidavits, customs correspondence, and
        parish records in the Essex Records
        Office, Chelmsford

INDEX

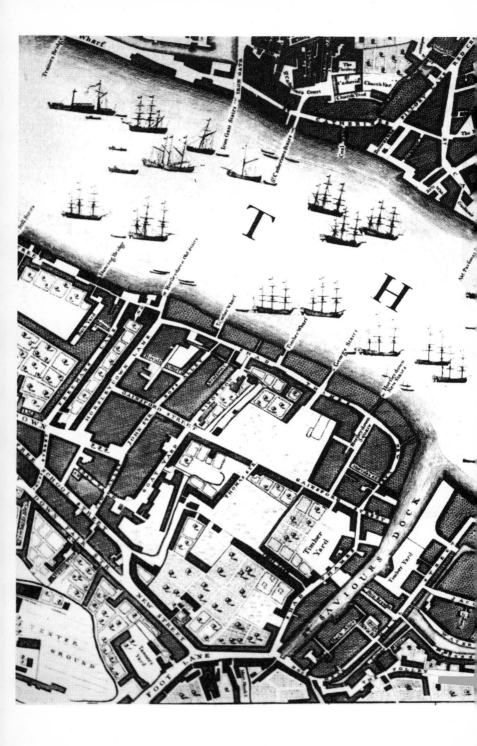